GNU COBOL 2.1 Quick Reference

A catalogue record for this book is available from the Hong Kong Public Libraries.

Published in Hong Kong by Samurai Media Limited.

Email: info@samuraimedia.org

ISBN 978-988-8406-25-8

Table of Contents

1. CDF 1

2. IDENTIFICATION DIVISION Syntax 5

3. ENVIRONMENT DIVISION Syntax 7

4. DATA DIVISION Syntax 15

5. PROCEDURE DIVISION Syntax 27

6. Intrinsic Functions Syntax 63

7. Built-In Subroutines Syntax 75

8. GNU Free Documentation License 81

1. CDF

```
                          CDF COPY Statement Syntax

COPY copybook-name
~~~~

[ IN|OF library-name ]
  ~~ ~~

[ SUPPRESS PRINTING ]
  ~~~~~~~~

[ REPLACING { Phrase-Clause | String-Clause }... ]  .
  ~~~~~~~~
```

```
                        CDF COPY Phrase-Clause Syntax

{ ==pseudo-text-1== } BY { ==pseudo-text-2== }
{ identifier-1      } ~~ { identifier-2       }
{ literal-1         }    { literal-2          }
{ word-1            }    { word-2             }
```

```
                        CDF COPY String-Clause Syntax

[ LEADING|TRAILING ] ==partial-word-1== BY ==partial-word-2==
  ~~~~~~~ ~~~~~~~~                       ~~
```

```
                   CDF REPLACE Statement (Format 1) Syntax

REPLACE [ ALSO ] { Phrase-Clause | String-Clause }...  .
~~~~~~~   ~~~~
```

```
                   CDF REPLACE Statement (Format 2) Syntax

REPLACE [ LAST ] OFF .
~~~~~~~   ~~~~   ~~~
```

```
                      CDF REPLACE Phrase-Clause Syntax

{ ==pseudo-text-1== } BY { ==pseudo-text-2 }
                      ~~
```

```
                      CDF REPLACE String-Clause Syntax

[ LEADING|TRAILING ] ==partial-word-1== BY ==partial-word-2==
  ~~~~~~~ ~~~~~~~~                       ~~
```

```
┌─────────────────────────────────────────────────────────────────────┐
│                    CDF >>DEFINE Directive Syntax                      │
└─────────────────────────────────────────────────────────────────────┘

>>DEFINE [ CONSTANT ] cdf-variable-1 AS { OFF                       }
~~~~~~~~   ~~~~~~~~                      { ~~~                       }
                                        { literal-1 [ OVERRIDE ]    }
                                        {             ~~~~~~~~       }
                                        { PARAMETER [ OVERRIDE ]    }
                                          ~~~~~~~~~   ~~~~~~~~

┌─────────────────────────────────────────────────────────────────────┐
│                     CDF >>IF Directive Syntax                         │
└─────────────────────────────────────────────────────────────────────┘

>>IF CDF-Conditional-Expression-1
~~~~       [ Program-Source-Lines-1 ]

[ >>ELIF CDF-Conditional-Expression-2
  ~~~~~~   [ Program-Source-Lines-2 ] ]...

[ >>ELSE
  ~~~~~~   [ Program-Source-Lines-3 ] ]

>>END-IF
~~~~~~~~

┌─────────────────────────────────────────────────────────────────────┐
│                  CDF-Conditional-Expression Syntax                    │
└─────────────────────────────────────────────────────────────────────┘

{ cdf-variable-1 } IS [ NOT ] { DEFINED                        }
{ literal-1       }    ~~~     { ~~~~~~~                        }
                              { SET                            }
                              { ~~~                            }
                              { CDF-RelOp { cdf-variable-2 }   }
                              {           { literal-2       }  }

┌─────────────────────────────────────────────────────────────────────┐
│                        CDF-RelOp Syntax                               │
└─────────────────────────────────────────────────────────────────────┘

>=    or    GREATER THAN OR EQUAL TO
            ~~~~~~~      ~~ ~~~~~

>     or    GREATER THAN
            ~~~~~~~

<=    or    LESS THAN OR EQUAL TO
            ~~~~      ~~ ~~~~~

<     or    LESS THAN
            ~~~~

=     or    EQUAL TO
            ~~~~~

<>    or    EQUAL TO (with "NOT")
            ~~~~~
```

CDF >>SET Directive Syntax

```
>>SET { [ CONSTANT ] cdf-variable-1 [ AS literal-1 ] }
~~~~~ {     ~~~~~~~~                      ~~          }
      { SOURCEFORMAT AS FIXED|FREE                   }
      { ~~~~~~~~~~~~     ~~~~~ ~~~~                   }
      { NOFOLDCOPYNAME                               }
      { ~~~~~~~~~~~~~~                               }
      { FOLDCOPYNAME AS UPPER|LOWER                  }
        ~~~~~~~~~~~~     ~~~~~ ~~~~~
```

CDF >>SOURCE Directive Syntax

```
>>SOURCE FORMAT IS FIXED|FREE
~~~~~~~~            ~~~~~ ~~~~
```

CDF >>TURN Directive Syntax

```
>>TURN { exception-name-1 [ file-name-1 ]...  }...
~~~~~~
       { OFF                            }
       { ~~~                            }
       { CHECKING ON [ WITH LOCATION ] }
         ~~~~~~~~ ~~        ~~~~~~~~
```

The ">>TURN" CDF directive is syntactically recognized but is otherwise non-functional.

2. IDENTIFICATION DIVISION Syntax

IDENTIFICATION DIVISION Syntax

```
[ IDENTIFICATION DIVISION. ]
  ~~~~~~~~~~~~~~ ~~~~~~~~

{ PROGRAM-ID.  } program-id [ AS literal-1 ] [ Type-Clause ] .
{ ~~~~~~~~~~   }
{ FUNCTION-ID. }
  ~~~~~~~~~~~

[ AUTHOR. comment-1.  ]
  ~~~~~~

[ DATE-COMPILED. comment-2.  ]
  ~~~~~~~~~~~~~

[ DATE-WRITTEN. comment-3.  ]
  ~~~~~~~~~~~~

[ INSTALLATION. comment-4.  ]
  ~~~~~~~~~~~~

[ REMARKS. comment-5.  ]
  ~~~~~~~

[ SECURITY. comment-6.  ]
  ~~~~~~~~
```

The "AUTHOR", "DATE-COMPILED", "DATE-WRITTEN", "INSTALLATION", "REMARKS" and "SECURITY" paragraphs are supported by GNU COBOL only to provide compatibility with programs written for the ANS1974 (or earlier) standards. As of the ANS1985 standard, these clauses have become obsolete and should not be used in new programs.

PROGRAM-ID Type Clause Syntax

```
IS [ COMMON ] [ INITIAL|RECURSIVE PROGRAM ]
   ~~~~~~       ~~~~~~~ ~~~~~~~~~
```

3. ENVIRONMENT DIVISION Syntax

ENVIRONMENT DIVISION Syntax

```
ENVIRONMENT DIVISION.
~~~~~~~~~~~ ~~~~~~~~
[ CONFIGURATION SECTION. ]
~~~~~~~~~~~~~ ~~~~~~~
[ SOURCE-COMPUTER.       Compilation-Computer-Specification . ]
~~~~~~~~~~~~~~~
[ OBJECT-COMPUTER.       Execution-Computer-Specification . ]
~~~~~~~~~~~~~~~
[ REPOSITORY.            Function-Specification... . ]
~~~~~~~~~~
[ SPECIAL-NAMES.         Program-Configuration-Specification . ]
~~~~~~~~~~~~~
[ INPUT-OUTPUT SECTION. ]
~~~~~~~~~~~~ ~~~~~~~
[ FILE-CONTROL.          General-File-Description... . ]
~~~~~~~~~~~~
[ I-O-CONTROL.           File-Buffering Specification... . ]
~~~~~~~~~~
```

CONFIGURATION SECTION Syntax

```
CONFIGURATION SECTION.
~~~~~~~~~~~~~ ~~~~~~~
[ SOURCE-COMPUTER. Compilation-Computer-Specification . ]
~~~~~~~~~~~~~~~
[ OBJECT-COMPUTER. Execution-Computer-Specification . ]
~~~~~~~~~~~~~~~
[ REPOSITORY.      Function-Specification... . ]
~~~~~~~~~~
[ SPECIAL-NAMES.   Program-Configuration-Specification . ]
~~~~~~~~~~~~~
```

SOURCE-COMPUTER Syntax

```
SOURCE-COMPUTER. computer-name [ WITH DEBUGGING MODE ] .
~~~~~~~~~~~~~~~                      ~~~~~~~~~ ~~~~
```

OBJECT-COMPUTER Syntax

```
OBJECT-COMPUTER.   [ computer-name ]
~~~~~~~~~~~~~~~

[ MEMORY SIZE IS integer-1 WORDS|CHARACTERS ]
  ~~~~~~ ~~~~               ~~~~~ ~~~~~~~~~~

[ PROGRAM COLLATING SEQUENCE IS alphabet-name-1 ]
          ~~~~~~~~~

[ SEGMENT-LIMIT IS integer-2 ]
  ~~~~~~~~~~~~~

[ CHARACTER CLASSIFICATION IS { locale-name-1  } ]
            ~~~~~~~~~~~~~~      { LOCALE         }
                                { ~~~~~~         }
                                { USER-DEFAULT   }
                                { ~~~~~~~~~~~~    }
                                { SYSTEM-DEFAULT }
                                  ~~~~~~~~~~~~~~
```

.

The "MEMORY SIZE" and "SEGMENT-LIMIT" clauses are syntactically recognized but are otherwise non-functional.

REPOSITORY Syntax

```
REPOSITORY.
~~~~~~~~~~

    FUNCTION { function-prototype-name-1 [ AS literal-1 ] }...
    ~~~~~~~~ {                             ~~            }
             { intrinsic-function-name-1 [ AS literal-2 ] }
             {                             ~~            }
             { intrinsic-function-name-2 INTRINSIC       }
             { ALL INTRINSIC              ~~~~~~~~~       }
               ~~~ ~~~~~~~~~
```

SPECIAL-NAMES Syntax

```
SPECIAL-NAMES.
~~~~~~~~~~~~~
  [ CALL-CONVENTION integer-1 IS mnemonic-name-1 ]
    ~~~~~~~~~~~~~~~~

  [ CONSOLE IS CRT ]
    ~~~~~~~    ~~~

  [ CRT STATUS IS identifier-1 ]
    ~~~ ~~~~~~

  [ CURRENCY SIGN IS literal-1 ]
    ~~~~~~~~ ~~~~

  [ CURSOR IS identifier-2 ]
    ~~~~~~

  [ DECIMAL-POINT IS COMMA ]
    ~~~~~~~~~~~~~    ~~~~~

  [ EVENT STATUS IS identifier-3 ]
    ~~~~~ ~~~~~~

  [ LOCALE locale-name-1 IS literal-2 ]...
    ~~~~~~

  [ NUMERIC SIGN IS TRAILING SEPARATE ]
    ~~~~~~~ ~~~~    ~~~~~~~~ ~~~~~~~~

  [ SCREEN CONTROL IS identifier-4 ]
    ~~~~~~ ~~~~~~~

  [ device-name-1 IS mnemonic-name-2 ]...

  [ feature-name-1 IS mnemonic-name-3 ]...

  [ Alphabet-Clause ]...

  [ Class-Definition-Clause ]...

  [ Switch-Definition-Clause ]...

  [ Symbolic-Characters-Clause ]...
  .
```

The "EVENT STATUS" and "SCREEN CONTROL" clauses are syntactically recognized but are otherwise non-functional.

```
                        SPECIAL-NAMES Alphabet-Clause Syntax
```

```
ALPHABET alphabet-name-1 IS { ASCII             }
~~~~~~~~                     { ~~~~~             }
                            { EBCDIC            }
                            { ~~~~~~            }
                            { NATIVE            }
                            { ~~~~~~            }
                            { STANDARD-1        }
                            { ~~~~~~~~~~        }
                            { STANDARD-2        }
                            { ~~~~~~~~~~        }
                            { Literal-Clause... }
```

```
                     SPECIAL-NAMES ALPHABET Literal-Clause Syntax
```

```
literal-1 [ { THRU|THROUGH literal-2 } ]
            { ~~~~ ~~~~~~~            }
            { {ALSO literal-3}...     }
              ~~~~
```

```
                   SPECIAL-NAMES Class-Definition-Clause Syntax
```

```
CLASS class-name-1 IS { literal-1 [ THRU|THROUGH literal-2 ] }...
~~~~~                              ~~~~ ~~~~~~~
```

```
                   SPECIAL-NAMES Switch-Definition-Clause Syntax
```

```
switch-name-1 [ IS mnemonic-name-1 ]

  [ ON STATUS IS condition-name-1 ]
    ~~

  [ OFF STATUS IS condition-name-2 ]
    ~~~
```

```
                 SPECIAL-NAMES-Symbolic-Characters-Clause Syntax
```

```
SYMBOLIC CHARACTERS
~~~~~~~~

  { symbolic-character-1...  IS|ARE integer-1...  }...

  [ IN alphabet-name-1 ]
    ~~
```

INPUT-OUTPUT SECTION Syntax

```
[ INPUT-OUTPUT SECTION. ]
  ~~~~~~~~~~~~ ~~~~~~~

[ FILE-CONTROL. ]
  ~~~~~~~~~~~~

    [ SELECT-Statement... ]

[ I-O-CONTROL. ]
  ~~~~~~~~~~~

    [ MULTIPLE-FILE-Statement ]

    [ SAME-RECORD-Statement ]
```

I-O-CONTROL MULTIPLE FILE Syntax

```
MULTIPLE FILE TAPE CONTAINS
~~~~~~~~

    { file-name-1 [ POSITION integer-1 ] }...
                    ~~~~~~~~

    .
```

The "MULTIPLE FILE TAPE" clause is obsolete and is therefore recognized but not functional.

I-O-CONTROL SAME AREA Syntax

```
SAME { SORT-MERGE } AREA FOR file-name-1...   .
~~~~ { ~~~~~~~~~~ }
     { SORT        }
     { ~~~~        }
     { RECORD      }
       ~~~~~~
```

The "SAME SORT-MERGE" and "SAME SORT" clauses are syntactically recognized but are otherwise non-functional.

```
╭──────────────────────────────────────────────────────────────────────────╮
│                          SELECT Statement Syntax                           │
╰──────────────────────────────────────────────────────────────────────────╯

SELECT [ [ NOT ] OPTIONAL ] file-name-1
~~~~~~      ~~~   ~~~~~~~~

[ ASSIGN { TO    } [{ EXTERNAL }] [{ DISC|DISK      }] [{ identifier-1 }] ]
  ~~~~~~ { USING }  { ~~~~~~~~ }   { ~~~~ ~~~~       }   { word-1       }
                   { DYNAMIC  }   { DISPLAY         }   { literal-1    }
                     ~~~~~~~       { ~~~~~~~         }
                                  { KEYBOARD        }
                                  { ~~~~~~~~        }
                                  { LINE ADVANCING  }
                                  { ~~~~ ~~~~~~~~~  }
                                  { PRINTER         }
                                  { ~~~~~~~         }
                                  { RANDOM          }
                                  { ~~~~~~          }
                                  { TAPE            }
                                    ~~~~

[ COLLATING SEQUENCE IS alphabet-name-1 ]
           ~~~~~~~~~

[ FILE|SORT ] STATUS IS identifier-2 [ identifier-3 ] ]
  ~~~~ ~~~~   ~~~~~~

[ LOCK MODE IS { MANUAL|AUTOMATIC                             } ]
  ~~~~         { ~~~~~~ ~~~~~~~~~                              }
              { EXCLUSIVE [ WITH { LOCK ON MULTIPLE RECORDS } ] }
                ~~~~~~~~~         { ~~~~ ~~ ~~~~~~~~ ~~~~~~~ }
                                 { LOCK ON RECORD           }
[ ORGANIZATION-Clause ]          { ~~~~ ~~ ~~~~~~           }
                                 { ROLLBACK                 }
[ RECORD DELIMITER IS STANDARD-1 ] ~~~~~~~~
  ~~~~~~ ~~~~~~~~~    ~~~~~~~~~~

[ RESERVE integer-1 AREAS ]
  ~~~~~~~

[ SHARING WITH { ALL OTHER } ]
  ~~~~~~~      { ~~~       }
              { NO OTHER  }
              { ~~        }
              { READ ONLY }
                ~~~~ ~~~~
```

The "COLLATING SEQUENCE", "RECORD DELIMITER", "RESERVE" and "ALL OTHER" clauses
are syntactically recognized but are otherwise non-functional.

```
┌─────────────────────────────────────────────────────────────┐
│              ORGANIZATION SEQUENTIAL Clause Syntax             │
└─────────────────────────────────────────────────────────────┘
```

```
[ ORGANIZATION|ORGANISATION IS ] RECORD BINARY SEQUENTIAL
  ~~~~~~~~~~~~ ~~~~~~~~~~~~                 ~~~~~~~~~~

    [ ACCESS MODE IS SEQUENTIAL ]
      ~~~~~~      ~~~~~~~~~~
```

```
┌─────────────────────────────────────────────────────────────┐
│            ORGANIZATION LINE SEQUENTIAL Clause Syntax          │
└─────────────────────────────────────────────────────────────┘
```

```
[ ORGANIZATION|ORGANISATION IS ] LINE SEQUENTIAL
  ~~~~~~~~~~~~ ~~~~~~~~~~~~       ~~~~ ~~~~~~~~~~

    [ ACCESS MODE IS SEQUENTIAL ]
      ~~~~~~      ~~~~~~~~~~

    [ PADDING CHARACTER IS literal-1 | identifier-1 ]
      ~~~~~~~
```

The "PADDING CHARACTER" clause is syntactically recognized but is otherwise non-functional.

```
┌─────────────────────────────────────────────────────────────┐
│               ORGANIZATION RELATIVE Clause Syntax             │
└─────────────────────────────────────────────────────────────┘
```

```
[ ORGANIZATION|ORGANISATION IS ] RELATIVE
  ~~~~~~~~~~~~ ~~~~~~~~~~~~       ~~~~~~~~

    [ ACCESS MODE IS { SEQUENTIAL } ]
      ~~~~~~           { ~~~~~~~~~~ }
                       { DYNAMIC    }
                       { ~~~~~~~    }
                       { RANDOM     }
                         ~~~~~~

    [ RELATIVE KEY IS identifier-1 ]
      ~~~~~~~~
```

ORGANIZATION INDEXED Clause Syntax

```
[ ORGANIZATION|ORGANISATION IS ] INDEXED
  ~~~~~~~~~~~~ ~~~~~~~~~~~~        ~~~~~~~

    [ ACCESS MODE IS { SEQUENTIAL } ]
      ~~~~~~          { ~~~~~~~~~~ }
                      { DYNAMIC    }
                      { ~~~~~~~    }
                      { RANDOM     }
                        ~~~~~~

    [ RECORD KEY IS identifier-1
      ~~~~~~

           [ =|{SOURCE IS} identifier-2 ] ]
                 ~~~~~~

    [ ALTERNATE RECORD KEY IS identifier-3
      ~~~~~~~~~ ~~~~~~

           [ =|{SOURCE IS} identifier-4 ]
                 ~~~~~~

           [ WITH DUPLICATES ] ]...
                  ~~~~~~~~~~
```

The "SOURCE" clause is syntactically recognized but is otherwise non-functional. It is supported to provide compatibility with COBOL source written for other COBOL implementations.

4. DATA DIVISION Syntax

```
┌─────────────────────────────────────────────────────────────────────────┐
│                          DATA DIVISION Syntax                             │
└─────────────────────────────────────────────────────────────────────────┘

  DATA DIVISION.
  ~~~~ ~~~~~~~~

[ FILE SECTION.
  ~~~~ ~~~~~~~
  { File/Sort-Description [ { FILE-SECTION-Data-Item } ]... }... ]
  {                          { 01-Level-Constant       }      }
  {                          { 78-Level-Constant       }      }
  { 01-Level-Constant                                         }
  { 78-Level-Constant                                         }
[ WORKING-STORAGE SECTION.
  ~~~~~~~~~~~~~~~ ~~~~~~~
    [ { WORKING-STORAGE-SECTION-Data-Item } ]... ]
    { 01-Level-Constant                   }
    { 78-Level-Constant                   }
[ LOCAL-STORAGE SECTION.
  ~~~~~~~~~~~~~ ~~~~~~~
    [ { LOCAL-STORAGE-SECTION-Data-Item } ]... ]
    { 01-Level-Constant                 }
    { 78-Level-Constant                 }
[ LINKAGE SECTION.
  ~~~~~~~ ~~~~~~~
    [ { LINKAGE-SECTION-Data-Item } ]... ]
    { 01-Level-Constant           }
    { 78-Level-Constant           }
[ REPORT SECTION.
  ~~~~~~ ~~~~~~~
  { Report-Description [ { Report-Group-Definition } ]... }... ]
  {                      { 01-Level-Constant        }      }
  {                      { 78-Level-Constant        }      }
  { 01-Level-Constant                                      }
  { 78-Level-Constant                                      }
[ SCREEN SECTION.
  ~~~~~~ ~~~~~~~
   [ { SCREEN-SECTION-Data-Item } ]... ]
   { 01-Level-Constant          }
   { 78-Level-Constant          }
```

File/Sort-Description Syntax

```
FD|SD file-name-1 [ IS EXTERNAL|GLOBAL ]
~~ ~~                 ~~~~~~~~ ~~~~~~

[ BLOCK CONTAINS [ integer-1 TO ] integer-2 CHARACTERS|RECORDS ]
  ~~~~~                      ~~              ~~~~~~~~~~ ~~~~~~~

[ CODE-SET IS alphabet-name-1 ]
  ~~~~~~~~

[ DATA { RECORD IS  } identifier-1...  ]
  ~~~~ { ~~~~~~      }
       { RECORDS ARE }
         ~~~~~~~

[ LABEL { RECORD IS   } OMITTED|STANDARD ]
  ~~~~~ { ~~~~~~       } ~~~~~~~ ~~~~~~~~
        { RECORDS ARE }
          ~~~~~~~

[ LINAGE IS integer-3 | identifier-2 LINES
  ~~~~~~

    [ LINES AT BOTTOM integer-4 | identifier-3 ]
              ~~~~~~

    [ LINES AT TOP integer-5 | identifier-4 ]
              ~~~

    [ WITH FOOTING AT integer-6 | identifier-5 ] ]
           ~~~~~~~

[ RECORD { CONTAINS [ integer-7 TO ] integer-8 CHARACTERS   } ]
  ~~~~~~ {                      ~~                           }
         { IS VARYING IN SIZE                                }
         {    ~~~~~~~                                        }
         {      [ FROM [ integer-7 TO ] integer-8 CHARACTERS }
         {                       ~~                          }
         {            DEPENDING ON identifier-6 ]            }
                      ~~~~~~~~~

[ RECORDING MODE IS recording-mode ]
  ~~~~~~~~~

[ { REPORT IS   } report-name-1...  ]
  { ~~~~~~       }
  { REPORTS ARE }
    ~~~~~~~

[ VALUE OF implementor-name-1 IS literal-1 | identifier-7 ] .
  ~~~~~ ~~
```

The "BLOCK CONTAINS", "DATA RECORD", "LABEL RECORD", "RECORDING MODE" and "VALUE OF" clauses are syntactically recognized but are obsolete and non-functional. These clauses should not be coded in new programs.

```
┌─────────────────────────────────────────────────────────────────┐
│                    FILE-SECTION-Data-Item Syntax                  │
└─────────────────────────────────────────────────────────────────┘

 level-number [ identifier-1 | FILLER ] [ IS GLOBAL|EXTERNAL ]
                ~~~~~~                       ~~~~~~ ~~~~~~~~

 [ BLANK WHEN ZERO ]
   ~~~~~       ~~~~

 [ JUSTIFIED RIGHT ]
   ~~~~

 [ OCCURS [ integer-1 TO ] integer-2 TIMES
   ~~~~~~             ~~

        [ DEPENDING ON identifier-2 ]
          ~~~~~~~~~

        [ ASCENDING|DESCENDING KEY IS identifier-3 ]
          ~~~~~~~~~ ~~~~~~~~~~

        [ INDEXED BY identifier-4 ] ]
          ~~~~~~~

 [ PICTURE IS picture-string ]
   ~~~

 [ REDEFINES identifier-5 ]
   ~~~~~~~~~

 [ SIGN IS LEADING|TRAILING [ SEPARATE [CHARACTER] ] ]
   ~~~~    ~~~~~~~ ~~~~~~~~    ~~~~~~~~

 [ SYNCRONIZED|SYNCHRONISED [ LEFT|RIGHT ] ]
   ~~~~        ~~~~           ~~~~ ~~~~~

 [ USAGE IS data-item-usage ] .  [ FILE-SECTION-Data-Item ]...
   ~~~~~
```

The "LEFT" and "RIGHT" (SYNCRONIZED) clauses are syntactically recognized but are otherwise non-functional.

```
┌────────────────────────────────────────────────────────────────────┐
│              WORKING-STORAGE-SECTION-Data-Item Syntax                │
└────────────────────────────────────────────────────────────────────┘

   level-number [ identifier-1 | FILLER ] [ IS GLOBAL | EXTERNAL ]
                  ~~~~~~                        ~~~~~~   ~~~~~~~~

   [ BASED ]
     ~~~~~

   [ BLANK WHEN ZERO ]
     ~~~~~      ~~~~

   [ JUSTIFIED RIGHT ]
     ~~~~

   [ OCCURS [ integer-1 TO ] integer-2 TIMES
     ~~~~~~             ~~
         [ DEPENDING ON identifier-2 ]
           ~~~~~~~~~

         [ ASCENDING|DESCENDING KEY IS identifier-3 ]
           ~~~~~~~~~ ~~~~~~~~~~

         [ INDEXED BY identifier-4 ] ]
           ~~~~~~~

   [ PICTURE IS picture-string ]
     ~~~

   [ REDEFINES identifier-5 ]
     ~~~~~~~~~

   [ SIGN IS LEADING|TRAILING [ SEPARATE CHARACTER ] ]
     ~~~~    ~~~~~~~ ~~~~~~~~    ~~~~~~~~

   [ SYNCRONIZED|SYNCHRONISED [ LEFT|RIGHT ] ]
     ~~~~        ~~~~           ~~~~ ~~~~~

   [ USAGE IS data-item-usage ]
     ~~~~~

   [ VALUE IS [ ALL ] literal-1 ] .  [ WORKING-STORAGE-SECTION-Data-Item ]...
     ~~~~~        ~~~
```

The "LEFT" and "RIGHT" (SYNCRONIZED) clauses are syntactically recognized but are otherwise non-functional.

```
                    LOCAL-STORAGE-SECTION-Data-Item Syntax
```

```
level-number [ identifier-1 | FILLER ] [ IS GLOBAL|EXTERNAL ]
                 ~~~~~~                      ~~~~~~ ~~~~~~~~

[ BASED ]
  ~~~~~

[ BLANK WHEN ZERO ]
  ~~~~~      ~~~~

[ JUSTIFIED RIGHT ]
  ~~~~

[ OCCURS [ integer-1 TO ] integer-2 TIMES
  ~~~~~~            ~~

      [ DEPENDING ON identifier-2 ]
        ~~~~~~~~~

      [ ASCENDING|DESCENDING KEY IS identifier-3 ]
        ~~~~~~~~~ ~~~~~~~~~~

      [ INDEXED BY identifier-4 ] ]
        ~~~~~~~

[ PICTURE IS picture-string ]
  ~~~

[ REDEFINES identifier-5 ]
  ~~~~~~~~~

[ SIGN IS LEADING|TRAILING [ SEPARATE CHARACTER ] ]
  ~~~~    ~~~~~~~ ~~~~~~~~    ~~~~~~~

[ SYNCRONIZED|SYNCHRONISED [ LEFT|RIGHT ] ]
  ~~~~         ~~~~           ~~~~ ~~~~~

[ USAGE IS data-item-usage ]
  ~~~~~

[ VALUE IS [ ALL ] literal-1 ] .  [ LOCAL-STORAGE-SECTION-Data-Item ]...
  ~~~~~       ~~~
```

The "LEFT" and "RIGHT" (SYNCRONIZED) clauses are syntactically recognized but are otherwise non-functional.

LINKAGE-SECTION-Data-Item Syntax

```
level-number [ identifier-1 | FILLER ] [ IS GLOBAL|EXTERNAL ]

[ ANY LENGTH ]

[ BASED ]

[ BLANK WHEN ZERO ]

[ JUSTIFIED RIGHT ]

[ OCCURS [ integer-1 TO ] integer-2 TIMES

      [ DEPENDING ON identifier-3 ]

      [ ASCENDING|DESCENDING KEY IS identifier-4 ]

      [ INDEXED BY identifier-5 ] ]

[ PICTURE IS picture-string ]

[ REDEFINES identifier-6 ]

[ SIGN IS LEADING|TRAILING [ SEPARATE CHARACTER ] ]

[ SYNCRONIZED|SYNCHRONISED [ LEFT|RIGHT ] ]

[ USAGE IS data-item-usage ] .  [ LINKAGE-SECTION-Data-Item ]...
```

The "LEFT" and "RIGHT" (SYNCRONIZED) clauses are syntactically recognized but are otherwise non-functional.

Report-Description (RD) Syntax

```
RD report-name [ IS GLOBAL ]
~~                 ~~~~~~

[ CODE IS literal-1 | identifier-1 ]
  ~~~~

[ { CONTROL IS  } { FINAL        }... ]
  { ~~~~~~~      } { ~~~~~        }
  { CONTROLS ARE } { identifier-2 }
    ~~~~~~~~

[ PAGE [ { LIMIT IS  } ] [ { literal-2   } LINES ]
  ~~~~   { ~~~~~      }     { identifier-3 } ~~~~
         { LIMITS ARE }
           ~~~~~~

      [ literal-3 | identifier-4 COLUMNS|COLS ]
                                 ~~~~~~~ ~~~~

      [ HEADING IS literal-4 | identifier-5 ]
        ~~~~~~~

      [ FIRST DE|DETAIL IS literal-5 | identifier-6 ]
        ~~~~~ ~~ ~~~~~~

      [ LAST CH|{CONTROL HEADING} IS literal-6 | identifier-7 ]
        ~~~~ ~~  ~~~~~~~ ~~~~~~~

      [ LAST DE|DETAIL IS literal-7 | identifier-8 ]
        ~~~~ ~~ ~~~~~~

      [ FOOTING IS literal-8 | identifier-9 ] ] .
        ~~~~~~~
```

The "CODE IS" and "COLUMNS" clauses are syntactically recognized but are otherwise non-functional.

Report-Group-Definition Syntax

```
01 [ identifier-1 ]

[ LINE NUMBER IS { integer-1 [ [ ON NEXT PAGE ] } ]
  ~~~~               {                    ~~~~ ~~~~      }
                     { +|PLUS integer-1                 }
                     {     ~~~~                          }
                     { ON NEXT PAGE                     }
                       ~~~~ ~~~~

[ NEXT GROUP IS { [ +|PLUS ] integer-2  } ]
  ~~~~ ~~~~~       {        ~~~~              }
                  { NEXT|{NEXT PAGE}|PAGE }
                    ~~~~  ~~~~ ~~~~  ~~~~

[ TYPE IS { RH|{REPORT HEADING}                    } ]
  ~~~~       { ~~  ~~~~~~ ~~~~~~~                    }
             { PH|{PAGE HEADING}                    }
             { ~~  ~~~~ ~~~~~~~                      }
             { CH|{CONTROL HEADING} FINAL|identifier-2 }
             { ~~  ~~~~~~~ ~~~~~~~  ~~~~~            }
             { DE|DETAIL                            }
             { ~~ ~~~~~~                             }
             { CF|{CONTROL FOOTING} FINAL|identifier-2 }
             { ~~  ~~~~~~~ ~~~~~~~  ~~~~~            }
             { PF|{PAGE FOOTING}                    }
             {  ~~ ~~~~ ~~~~~~~                      }
             { RF|{REPORT FOOTING}                  }
               ~~  ~~~~~~ ~~~~~~~

.  [ REPORT-SECTION-Data-Item ]...
```

```
                     REPORT-SECTION-Data-Item Syntax

level-number [ identifier-1 ]

[ BLANK WHEN ZERO ]
  ~~~~~      ~~~~
[ COLUMN [ { NUMBER IS  } ] [ +|PLUS ] integer-1 ]
  ~~~      { ~~~~~~      }      ~~~~
           { NUMBERS ARE }
             ~~~~~~~
[ GROUP INDICATE ]
  ~~~~~ ~~~~~~~~
[ JUSTIFIED RIGHT ]
  ~~~~
[ LINE NUMBER IS { integer-2 [ [ ON NEXT PAGE ] } ]
  ~~~~           { +|PLUS integer-2 ~~~~ ~~~~    }
                 {   ~~~~                        }
                 { ON NEXT PAGE                  }
                   ~~~~ ~~~~
[ OCCURS [ integer-3 TO ] integer-4 TIMES
  ~~~~~~              ~~
     [ DEPENDING ON identifier-2 ]
       ~~~~~~~~~
     [ STEP integer-5 ]
       ~~~~
     [ VARYING identifier-3 FROM { identifier-4 } BY { identifier-5 } ]
       ~~~~~~~              ~~~~ { integer-6     } ~~ { integer-7     }
[ PICTURE IS picture-string ]
  ~~~
[ PRESENT WHEN condition-name ]
  ~~~~~~~ ~~~~
[ SIGN IS LEADING|TRAILING [ SEPARATE CHARACTER ] ]
  ~~~~    ~~~~~~~ ~~~~~~~~    ~~~~~~~~
[ { SOURCE IS literal-1|identifier-6 [ ROUNDED ]              } ]
  { ~~~~~~                             ~~~~~~~                }
  { SUM OF { identifier-7 }...  [ { RESET ON FINAL|identifier-8 } ] }
  { ~~~    { literal-2     }      { ~~~~~      ~~~~~             } }
  { VALUE IS [ ALL ] literal-3    { UPON identifier-9            } }
    ~~~~~      ~~~                  ~~~~
  . [ REPORT-SECTION-Data-Item ]...
```

SCREEN-SECTION-Data-Item Syntax

```
level-number [ identifier-1 | FILLER ]
                 ~~~~~~

[ AUTO | AUTO-SKIP | AUTOTERMINATE ] [ BELL | BEEP ]
  ~~~~   ~~~~~~~~~   ~~~~~~~~~~~~~     ~~~~   ~~~~

[ BACKGROUND-COLOR|BACKGROUND-COLOUR IS integer-1 | identifier-2 ]
  ~~~~~~~~~~~~~~~~ ~~~~~~~~~~~~~~~~~

[ BLANK LINE|SCREEN ] [ ERASE EOL|EOS ]
  ~~~~~ ~~~~ ~~~~~~     ~~~~~ ~~~ ~~~

[ BLANK WHEN ZERO ] [ JUSTIFIED RIGHT ]
  ~~~~~       ~~~~     ~~~~

[ BLINK ] [ HIGHLIGHT | LOWLIGHT ] [ REVERSE-VIDEO ]
  ~~~~~     ~~~~~~~~~   ~~~~~~~~     ~~~~~~~~~~~~~

[ COLUMN NUMBER IS [ +|PLUS ] integer-2 | identifier-3 ]
  ~~~                  ~~~~

[ FOREGROUND-COLOR|FOREGROUND-COLOUR IS integer-3 | identifier-4 ]
  ~~~~~~~~~~~~~~~~ ~~~~~~~~~~~~~~~~~

[ { FROM literal-1 | identifier-5 } ]
  { ~~~~                           }
  { TO identifier-5                }
  { ~~                             }
  { USING identifier-5             }
  { ~~~~~                          }
  { VALUE IS [ ALL ] literal-1     }
    ~~~~~       ~~~

[ FULL | LENGTH-CHECK ] [ REQUIRED | EMPTY-CHECK ] [ SECURE | NO-ECHO ]
  ~~~~   ~~~~~~~~~~~~     ~~~~~~~~   ~~~~~~~~~~~     ~~~~~~   ~~~~~~~

[ LEFTLINE ] [ OVERLINE ] [ UNDERLINE ]
  ~~~~~~~~     ~~~~~~~~     ~~~~~~~~~

[ LINE NUMBER IS [ +|PLUS ] integer-4 | identifier-6 ]
  ~~~~                ~~~~

[ OCCURS integer-5 TIMES ]
  ~~~~~~

[ PICTURE IS picture-string ]
  ~~~

[ PROMPT [ CHARACTER IS literal-2 | identifier-7 ]
  ~~~~~~   ~~~~~~~~~

[ SIGN IS LEADING|TRAILING [ SEPARATE CHARACTER ] ]
  ~~~~     ~~~~~~~ ~~~~~~~~    ~~~~~~~~

. [ SCREEN-SECTION-Data-Item ]...
```

```
                          01-Level-Constant Syntax
```

```
01 constant-name-1 CONSTANT [ IS GLOBAL ]
                   ~~~~~~~~~     ~~~~~~

  { AS { literal-1                          } } .
  {    { { BYTE-LENGTH } OF { identifier-1 } } }
  {    { { ~~~~~~~~~~~ }    { usage-name   } } }
  {    { { LENGTH      }                    } }
  {        ~~~~~~                            }
  { FROM CDF-variable-name-1                 }
    ~~~~
```

```
                          66-Level-Data-Item Syntax
```

```
66 identifier-1 RENAMES identifier-2 [ THRU|THROUGH identifier-3 ] .
                ~~~~~~~                 ~~~~ ~~~~~~~
```

```
                          77-Level-Data-Item Syntax
```

```
77 identifier-1 [ IS GLOBAL|EXTERNAL ]
                     ~~~~~~ ~~~~~~~~

[ BASED ]
  ~~~~~

[ BLANK WHEN ZERO ]
  ~~~~~      ~~~~

[ JUSTIFIED RIGHT ]
  ~~~~

[ PICTURE IS picture-string ]
  ~~~

[ REDEFINES identifier-5 ]
  ~~~~~~~~~

[ SIGN IS LEADING|TRAILING [ SEPARATE CHARACTER ] ]
  ~~~~      ~~~~~~~ ~~~~~~~~   ~~~~~~~~

[ SYNCRONIZED|SYNCHRONISED [ LEFT|RIGHT ] ]
  ~~~~         ~~~~           ~~~~ ~~~~~

[ USAGE IS data-item-usage ]
  ~~~~~

[ VALUE IS [ ALL ] literal-1 ] .
  ~~~~~        ~~~
```

The "LEFT" and "RIGHT" (SYNCRONIZED) clauses are syntactically recognized but are otherwise non-functional.

```
                          78-Level-Constant Syntax
```

```
78 constant-name-1 VALUE IS literal-1 .
                   ~~~~~
```

```
╭─────────────────────────────────────────────────────────────────────────────╮
│                          88-Level-Data-Item Syntax                            │
╰─────────────────────────────────────────────────────────────────────────────╯
88 condition-name-1 { VALUE IS  } {literal-1 [ THRU|THROUGH literal-2 ]}...
                     { ~~~~~     }            ~~~~ ~~~~~~~~
                     { VALUES ARE }
                       ~~~~~~

    [ WHEN SET TO FALSE IS literal-3 ] .
           ~~~~~
```

5. PROCEDURE DIVISION Syntax

PROCEDURE DIVISION Syntax

```
    PROCEDURE DIVISION [ { USING Subprogram-Argument ...     } ]
    ~~~~~~~~~ ~~~~~~~~   {  ~~~~~                             }
                        { CHAINING Main-Program-Argument...}
                          ~~~~~~~~

                        [ RETURNING identifier-1 ] .
[ DECLARATIVES. ]         ~~~~~~~~~
  ~~~~~~~~~~~~

[ Event-Handler-Routine...  .  ]

[ END DECLARATIVES. ]
  ~~~ ~~~~~~~~~~~~

    General-Program-Logic

[ Nested-Subprogram...  ]

[ END PROGRAM|FUNCTION name-1 ]
  ~~~ ~~~~~~~ ~~~~~~~~
```

PROCEDURE DIVISION Subprogram-Argument Syntax

```
[ BY { REFERENCE [ OPTIONAL ]                          } ] identifier-1
     {  ~~~~~~~~~   ~~~~~~~~                            }
     { VALUE [ [ UNSIGNED ] SIZE IS { AUTO      } ] }
       ~~~~~     ~~~~~~~~    ~~~~    {  ~~~~     }
                                    { DEFAULT   }
                                    {  ~~~~~~~   }
                                    { integer-1 }
```

PROCEDURE DIVISION Main-Program-Argument Syntax

```
[ BY REFERENCE ] [ OPTIONAL ] identifier-1
     ~~~~~~~~~       ~~~~~~~~
```

PROCEDURE DIVISION RETURNING Syntax

```
RETURNING identifier-1
~~~~~~~~~
```

```
┌─────────────────────────────────────────────────────────────────────────────┐
│                            DECLARATIVES Syntax                                │
└─────────────────────────────────────────────────────────────────────────────┘
```

```
section-name-1 SECTION.

USE { [ GLOBAL ] AFTER STANDARD { EXCEPTION } PROCEDURE ON { INPUT      } }
~~~ {   ~~~~~~                   { ~~~~~~~~~ }                { ~~~~~      } }
    {                           { ERROR     }                { OUTPUT     } }
    {                             ~~~~~                       { ~~~~~~     } }
    {                                                         { I-O        } }
    { FOR DEBUGGING ON { procedure-name-1          }          { ~~~        } }
    {     ~~~~~~~~~     { ALL PROCEDURES            }          { EXTEND     } }
    {                    { ~~~ ~~~~~~~~~~           }          { ~~~~~~     } }
    {                    { REFERENCES OF identifier-1 }        { file-name-1 } }
    {                                                                        }
    { [ GLOBAL ] BEFORE REPORTING identifier-2                              }
    {   ~~~~~~     ~~~~~~ ~~~~~~~~~                                          }
    {                                                                        }
    { AFTER EC|{EXCEPTION CONDITION}                                         }
      ~~    ~~~~~~~~~ ~~~~~~~~~
```

The "AFTER EXCEPTION CONDITION" and "AFTER EC" clauses are syntactically recognized
but are otherwise non-functional.

```
┌─────────────────────────────────────────────────────────────────────────────┐
│                              LENGTH OF Syntax                                 │
└─────────────────────────────────────────────────────────────────────────────┘
```

```
LENGTH OF numeric-literal-1 | identifier-1
~~~~~~
```

```
┌─────────────────────────────────────────────────────────────────────────────┐
│                    Reference Modifier (Format 1) Syntax                       │
└─────────────────────────────────────────────────────────────────────────────┘
```

```
identifier-1 [ OF|IN identifier-2 ] [ (subscript...) ]  (start:[ length ])
               ~~ ~~
```

```
┌─────────────────────────────────────────────────────────────────────────────┐
│                    Reference Modifier (Format 2) Syntax                       │
└─────────────────────────────────────────────────────────────────────────────┘
```

```
intrinsic-function-reference (start:[ length ])
```

```
┌─────────────────────────────────────────────────────────────────────────────┐
│                        Arithmetic-Expression Syntax                           │
└─────────────────────────────────────────────────────────────────────────────┘
```

```
Unary-Expression-1 { **|^ } Unary-Expression-2
                   { *|/ }
                   { +|- }
```

```
                          Unary-Expression Syntax

{ [ +|- ] { ( Arithmetic-Expression-1 )         } }
{         { [ LENGTH OF ] { identifier-1        } } }
{         {   ~~~~~~ ~~   { literal-1           } } }
{         {               { Function-Reference } } }
{ Arithmetic-Expression-2                       }
```

```
                          Class-Condition Syntax

identifier-1 IS [ NOT ] { NUMERIC          }
                  ~~~   { ~~~~~~~          }
                        { ALPHABETIC       }
                        { ~~~~~~~~~~       }
                        { ALPHABETIC-LOWER }
                        { ~~~~~~~~~~~~~~~~ }
                        { ALPHABETIC-UPPER }
                        { ~~~~~~~~~~~~~~~~ }
                        { OMITTED          }
                        { ~~~~~~~          }
                        { class-name-1     }
```

```
                          Sign-Condition Syntax

identifier-1 IS [ NOT ] { POSITIVE }
                  ~~~   { ~~~~~~~~ }
                        { NEGATIVE }
                        { ~~~~~~~~ }
                        { ZERO     }
                          ~~~~
```

```
                          Relation-Condition Syntax

{ identifier-1            } IS [ NOT ] RelOp { identifier-2            }
{ literal-1               }      ~~~         { literal-2               }
{ arithmetic-expression-1 }                 { arithmetic-expression-2 }
{ index-name-1            }                 { index-name-2            }
```

```
                              RelOp Syntax
```

```
{ EQUAL TO                }
{ ~~~~~                    }
{ EQUALS                   }
{ ~~~~~~                   }
{ GREATER THAN             }
{ ~~~~~~~                  }
{ GREATER THAN OR EQUAL TO }
{ ~~~~~~~         ~~ ~~~~~ }
{ LESS THAN                }
{ ~~~~                     }
{ LESS THAN OR EQUAL TO    }
{ ~~~~         ~~ ~~~~~    }
{ =                        }
{ >                        }
{ >=                       }
{ <                        }
{ <=                       }
```

```
                         Combined Condition Syntax
```

```
[ ( ] Condition-1 [ ) ] { AND } [ ( ] Condition-2 [ ) ]
                        { ~~~ }
                        { OR  }
                        { ~~  }
```

```
                          Negated Condition Syntax
```

```
NOT Condition-1
~~~
```

```
                        ACCEPT FROM CONSOLE Syntax
```

```
  ACCEPT identifier-1
  ~~~~~~

    [ FROM mnemonic-name-1 ]
      ~~~~

[ END-ACCEPT ]
  ~~~~~~~~~~
```

ACCEPT FROM COMMAND-LINE Syntax

```
ACCEPT identifier-1
~~~~~~
        FROM { COMMAND-LINE                                   }
        ~~~~ { ~~~~~~~~~~~~                                   }
             { ARGUMENT-NUMBER                                }
             { ~~~~~~~~~~~~~~~                                }
             { ARGUMENT-VALUE                                 }
             { ~~~~~~~~~~~~~~                                 }
             { [ ON EXCEPTION imperative-statement-1 ]        }
             {      ~~~~~~~~~                                 }
             { [ NOT ON EXCEPTION imperative-statement-2 ] }
[ END-ACCEPT ]       ~~~     ~~~~~~~~~
~~~~~~~~~~
```

ACCEPT FROM ENVIRONMENT Syntax

```
ACCEPT identifier-1
~~~~~~
        FROM { ENVIRONMENT-VALUE              }
        ~~~~ { ~~~~~~~~~~~~~~~~~              }
             { ENVIRONMENT { literal-1    } }
             { ~~~~~~~~~~~ { identifier-1 } }
        [ ON EXCEPTION imperative-statement-1 ]
             ~~~~~~~~~

        [ NOT ON EXCEPTION imperative-statement-2 ]
          ~~~     ~~~~~~~~~

[ END-ACCEPT ]
~~~~~~~~~~
```

```
┌─────────────────────────────────────────────────────────────────────────────┐
│                        ACCEPT screen-data-item Syntax                          │
└─────────────────────────────────────────────────────────────────────────────┘

    ACCEPT identifier-1 [ FROM CRT ] [ MODE IS BLOCK ]
    ~~~~~~              ~~~~ ~~~       ~~~~    ~~~~~
            [ AT { | LINE NUMBER { integer-1    }            | } ]
              ~~ { | ~~~~          { identifier-2 }           | }
                 { | COLUMN|POSITION NUMBER { integer-2   } | }
                 { | ~~~~~~ ~~~~~~~~~          { identifier-3 } | }
                 {                                              }
                 { { integer-3    }                            }
                 { { identifier-4 }                            }

            [ WITH [ Attribute-Specification ]...
              ~~~~
                    [ LOWER|UPPER ]
                      ~~~~~ ~~~~~

                    [ SCROLL { UP   } [ { integer-4    } LINE|LINES ] ]
                      ~~~~~~ { ~~   }   { identifier-5 }
                             { DOWN }
                               ~~~~

                    [ TIMEOUT|TIME-OUT AFTER { integer-5    } ]
                      ~~~~~~~ ~~~~~~~~        { identifier-6 }
                    [ CONVERSION ]
                      ~~~~~~~~~~~

                    [ UPDATE ] ]
                      ~~~~~~

            [ ON EXCEPTION imperative-statement-1 ]
                 ~~~~~~~~~

            [ NOT ON EXCEPTION imperative-statement-2 ]
              ~~~    ~~~~~~~~~
    [ END-ACCEPT ]
      ~~~~~~~~~~
```

The "FROM CRT", "MODE IS BLOCK", "CONVERSION" and "UPDATE" clauses are syntactically
recognized but are otherwise non-functional.

```
┌─────────────────────────────────────────────────────────────┐
│                 ACCEPT FROM DATE/TIME Syntax                  │
└─────────────────────────────────────────────────────────────┘

   ACCEPT identifier-1 FROM { DATE [ YYYYMMDD ] }
   ~~~~~~                ~~~~ {  ~~~~    ~~~~~~~~   }
                             { DAY [ YYYYDDD ]   }
                             {  ~~~    ~~~~~~~    }
                             { DAY-OF-WEEK       }
                             {  ~~~~~~~~~~~       }
   [ END-ACCEPT ]            { TIME              }
     ~~~~~~~~~~
```

```
┌─────────────────────────────────────────────────────────────┐
│                 ACCEPT FROM Screen-Info Syntax                │
└─────────────────────────────────────────────────────────────┘

   ACCEPT identifier-1
   ~~~~~~

        FROM { LINES|LINE-NUMBER }
        ~~~~ {  ~~~~~ ~~~~~~~~~~~  }
             { COLS|COLUMNS       }
             {  ~~~~ ~~~~~~~       }
             { ESCAPE KEY         }
               ~~~~~~ ~~~

   [ END-ACCEPT ]
     ~~~~~~~~~~
```

```
┌─────────────────────────────────────────────────────────────┐
│                ACCEPT FROM Runtime-Info Syntax                │
└─────────────────────────────────────────────────────────────┘

   ACCEPT identifier-1
   ~~~~~~

        FROM { EXCEPTION STATUS }
        ~~~~ {  ~~~~~~~~~ ~~~~~~  }
             { USER NAME        }
               ~~~~ ~~~~

   [ END-ACCEPT ]
     ~~~~~~~~~~
```

```
┌─────────────────────────────────────────────────────────────────┐
│                          ADD TO Syntax                            │
└─────────────────────────────────────────────────────────────────┘
```

```
ADD { literal-1    }...
~~~ { identifier-1 }

    TO { identifier-2
    ~~
        [ ROUNDED [ MODE IS { AWAY-FROM-ZERO          } ] ] }...
          ~~~~~~~   ~~~~    { ~~~~~~~~~~~~~            }
                            { NEAREST-AWAY-FROM-ZERO   }
                            { ~~~~~~~~~~~~~~~~~~~~~~    }
                            { NEAREST-EVEN             }
                            { ~~~~~~~~~~~~             }
                            { NEAREST-TOWARD-ZERO      }
                            { ~~~~~~~~~~~~~~~~~~~       }
                            { PROHIBITED               }
                            { ~~~~~~~~~~               }
                            { TOWARD-GREATER           }
                            { ~~~~~~~~~~~~~~            }
                            { TOWARD-LESSER            }
                            { ~~~~~~~~~~~~~             }
                            { TRUNCATION               }
                              ~~~~~~~~~~

    [ ON SIZE ERROR imperative-statement-1 ]
         ~~~~ ~~~~~

    [ NOT ON SIZE ERROR imperative-statement-2 ]
      ~~~    ~~~~ ~~~~~

[ END-ADD ]
  ~~~~~~~
```

```
┌─────────────────────────────────────────────────────────────────────┐
│                          ADD GIVING Syntax                            │
└─────────────────────────────────────────────────────────────────────┘

  ADD { literal-1    }...
  ~~~ { identifier-1 }

    [ TO identifier-2 ]
      ~~

      GIVING { identifier-3
      ~~~~~~

        [ ROUNDED [ MODE IS { AWAY-FROM-ZERO         } ] ] }...
          ~~~~~~~   ~~~~      { ~~~~~~~~~~~~~          }
                            { NEAREST-AWAY-FROM-ZERO }
                            { ~~~~~~~~~~~~~~~~~~~~~~  }
                            { NEAREST-EVEN           }
                            { ~~~~~~~~~~~~           }
                            { NEAREST-TOWARD-ZERO    }
                            { ~~~~~~~~~~~~~~~~~~~     }
                            { PROHIBITED             }
                            { ~~~~~~~~~~             }
                            { TOWARD-GREATER         }
                            { ~~~~~~~~~~~~~~         }
                            { TOWARD-LESSER          }
                            { ~~~~~~~~~~~~~          }
                            { TRUNCATION             }
                            ~~~~~~~~~~

    [ ON SIZE ERROR imperative-statement-1 ]
      ~~~~ ~~~~~

    [ NOT ON SIZE ERROR imperative-statement-2 ]
      ~~~    ~~~~ ~~~~~

  [ END-ADD ]
    ~~~~~~~
```

```
┌──────────────────────────────────────────────────────────────────┐
│                    ADD CORRESPONDING Syntax                        │
└──────────────────────────────────────────────────────────────────┘

ADD CORRESPONDING identifier-1
~~~

    TO identifier-2
    ~~

    [ ROUNDED [ MODE IS { AWAY-FROM-ZERO          } ] ]
      ~~~~~~~   ~~~~     { ~~~~~~~~~~~~~~          }
                        { NEAREST-AWAY-FROM-ZERO  }
                        { ~~~~~~~~~~~~~~~~~~~~~~~  }
                        { NEAREST-EVEN            }
                        { ~~~~~~~~~~~~            }
                        { NEAREST-TOWARD-ZERO     }
                        { ~~~~~~~~~~~~~~~~~~~      }
                        { PROHIBITED              }
                        { ~~~~~~~~~~              }
                        { TOWARD-GREATER          }
                        { ~~~~~~~~~~~~~~          }
                        { TOWARD-LESSER           }
                        { ~~~~~~~~~~~~~           }
                        { TRUNCATION              }
                          ~~~~~~~~~~

    [ ON SIZE ERROR imperative-statement-1 ]
      ~~~~ ~~~~~

    [ NOT ON SIZE ERROR imperative-statement-2 ]
      ~~~      ~~~~ ~~~~~

[ END-ADD ]
  ~~~~~~~
```

```
┌──────────────────────────────────────────────────────────────────┐
│                         ALLOCATE Syntax                            │
└──────────────────────────────────────────────────────────────────┘

ALLOCATE { expression-1 CHARACTERS } [ { INITIALIZED } ]
~~~~~~~~ { identifier-1 ~~~~~~~~~~ }   { ~~~~~~~~~~~ }
                                       { INITIALISED }
    [ RETURNING identifier-2 ]           ~~~~~~~~~~~
      ~~~~~~~~~
```

```
┌──────────────────────────────────────────────────────────────────┐
│                           ALTER Syntax                             │
└──────────────────────────────────────────────────────────────────┘

ALTER procedure-name-1 TO PROCEED TO procedure-name-2
~~~~~                     ~~
```

```
                              CALL Syntax
```

```
    CALL [ { STDCALL          } ] { literal-1     }
    ~~~~   { ~~~~~~~           }   { identifier-1 }
           { STATIC            }
           { ~~~~~~            }
           { mnemonic-name-1   }


           [ USING CALL-Argument... ]
             ~~~~~

           [ RETURNING|GIVING identifier-2 ]
             ~~~~~~~~~ ~~~~~~

           [ ON OVERFLOW|EXCEPTION imperative-statement-1 ]
                ~~~~~~~~ ~~~~~~~~~

           [ NOT ON OVERFLOW|EXCEPTION imperative-statement-2 ]
             ~~~      ~~~~~~~~ ~~~~~~~~~

   [ END-CALL ]
     ~~~~~~~~
```

```
                          CALL Argument Syntax
```

```
  [ BY { REFERENCE } ]
       { ~~~~~~~~~  }
       { CONTENT    }
       { ~~~~~~~    }
       { VALUE      }
         ~~~~~


       { OMITTED                                                }
       { ~~~~~~~                                                }
       { [ UNSIGNED ] [ SIZE IS { AUTO     } ] [ { literal-2   } }
           ~~~~~~~~        ~~~~  { ~~~~     }     { identifier-2 }
                                 { DEFAULT  }
                                 { ~~~~~~~  }
                                 { integer-1 }
```

```
                             CANCEL Syntax
```

```
  CANCEL { literal-1     }...
  ~~~~~~ { identifier-1 }
```

```
                              CLOSE Syntax
```

```
CLOSE { file-name-1 [ { REEL|UNIT [ FOR REMOVAL ] } ] }...
~~~~~                 { ~~~~ ~~~~          ~~~~~~~   }
                      { WITH LOCK                    }
                      {      ~~~~                     }
                      { WITH NO REWIND                }
                              ~~ ~~~~~~
```

The "REEL", "LOCK" and "NO REWIND" clauses are syntactically recognized but are otherwise
non-functional, except for the "CLOSE...NO REWIND" statement, which will generate a file
status of 07 rather than the usual 00 (but take no other action).

```
                              COMMIT Syntax
```

```
COMMIT
~~~~~~
```

```
                              COMPUTE Syntax
```

```
COMPUTE { identifier-1
~~~~~~~

        [ ROUNDED [ MODE IS { AWAY-FROM-ZERO         } ] }...
          ~~~~~~~    ~~~~    { ~~~~~~~~~~~~~~          }
                             { NEAREST-AWAY-FROM-ZERO }
                             { ~~~~~~~~~~~~~~~~~~~~~~  }
                             { NEAREST-EVEN           }
                             { ~~~~~~~~~~~~           }
                             { NEAREST-TOWARD-ZERO    }
                             { ~~~~~~~~~~~~~~~~~~~     }
                             { PROHIBITED             }
                             { ~~~~~~~~~~             }
                             { TOWARD-GREATER         }
                             { ~~~~~~~~~~~~~~         }
                             { TOWARD-LESSER          }
                             { ~~~~~~~~~~~~~          }
                             { TRUNCATION             }
                               ~~~~~~~~~~

        =|EQUAL arithmetic-expression-1
          ~~~~~

        [ ON SIZE ERROR imperative-statement-1 ]
          ~~~~ ~~~~~

        [ NOT ON SIZE ERROR imperative-statement-2 ]
          ~~~      ~~~~ ~~~~~

[ END-COMPUTE ]
  ~~~~~~~~~~~
```

CONTINUE Syntax

```
CONTINUE
~~~~~~~~
```

DELETE Syntax

```
  DELETE file-name-1 RECORD
  ~~~~~~

    [ INVALID KEY imperative-statement-1 ]
      ~~~~~~~

    [ NOT INVALID KEY imperative-statement-2 ]
      ~~~ ~~~~~~~

[ END-DELETE ]
  ~~~~~~~~~~
```

DISPLAY UPON device Syntax

```
  DISPLAY { literal-1    }...
  ~~~~~~~ { identifier-1 }
    [ UPON mnemonic-name-1 ]
      ~~~~

    [ WITH NO ADVANCING ]
           ~~ ~~~~~~~~~

    [ ON EXCEPTION imperative-statement-1 ]
         ~~~~~~~~~

    [ NOT ON EXCEPTION imperative-statement-2 ]
      ~~~    ~~~~~~~~~

[ END-DISPLAY ]
  ~~~~~~~~~~~
```

DISPLAY UPON COMMAND-LINE Syntax

```
  DISPLAY { literal-1    }...
  ~~~~~~~ { identifier-1 }
    UPON { ARGUMENT-NUMBER|COMMAND-LINE }
    ~~~~ { ~~~~~~~~~~~~~~~ ~~~~~~~~~~~~ }
    [ ON EXCEPTION imperative-statement-1 ]
         ~~~~~~~~~

    [ NOT ON EXCEPTION imperative-statement-2 ]
      ~~~    ~~~~~~~~~

[ END-DISPLAY ]
  ~~~~~~~~~~~
```

DISPLAY UPON ENVIRONMENT-NAME Syntax

```
DISPLAY { literal-1   }... UPON { ENVIRONMENT-VALUE }
~~~~~~~ { identifier-1 }   ~~~~ { ~~~~~~~~~~~~~~~~~ }
                                { ENVIRONMENT-NAME  }
                                  ~~~~~~~~~~~~~~~~

     [ ON EXCEPTION imperative-statement-1 ]
          ~~~~~~~~~

     [ NOT ON EXCEPTION imperative-statement-2 ]
       ~~~      ~~~~~~~~~

 [ END-DISPLAY ]
   ~~~~~~~~~~~
```

DISPLAY screen-data-item Syntax

```
DISPLAY identifier-1 [ UPON CRT|CRT-UNDER ]
~~~~~~~                ~~~~ ~~~ ~~~~~~~~~
     [ AT { | LINE NUMBER { integer-1   }          | } ]
       ~~ { | ~~~~        { identifier-2 }          | }
          { |                                       | }
          { | COLUMN|POSITION NUMBER { integer-2   } | } }
          { | ~~~~~~ ~~~~~~~~        { identifier-3 } | }
          {                                          }
          { { integer-3   }                          }
          { { identifier-4 }                          }

     [ WITH [ DISPLAY-Attribute ]...
       ~~~~

             [ SCROLL { UP   } [ { integer-4   } LINE|LINES ] ]
               ~~~~~~ { ~~   }  { identifier-5 }
                      { DOWN }
                        ~~~~

             [ TIMEOUT|TIME-OUT AFTER { integer-5   } ]
               ~~~~~~~ ~~~~~~~~       { identifier-6 }
             [ CONVERSION ] ]
               ~~~~~~~~~~

     [ ON EXCEPTION imperative-statement-1 ]
          ~~~~~~~~~

     [ NOT ON EXCEPTION imperative-statement-2 ]
       ~~~      ~~~~~~~~~

 [ END-DISPLAY ]
   ~~~~~~~~~~~
```

The "UPON CRT", "UPON CRT-UNDER" and "CONVERSION" clauses are syntactically recognized but are otherwise non-functional. They are supported to provide compatibility with COBOL source written for other COBOL implementations.

```
                            DIVIDE INTO Syntax
```

```
DIVIDE { literal-1    } INTO { identifier-2
~~~~~~ { identifier-1 } ~~~~

        [ ROUNDED [ MODE IS { AWAY-FROM-ZERO          } ] ] }...
          ~~~~~~~    ~~~~    { ~~~~~~~~~~~~~~          }
                            { NEAREST-AWAY-FROM-ZERO  }
                            { ~~~~~~~~~~~~~~~~~~~~~~~  }
                            { NEAREST-EVEN            }
                            { ~~~~~~~~~~~~            }
                            { NEAREST-TOWARD-ZERO     }
                            { ~~~~~~~~~~~~~~~~~~~      }
                            { PROHIBITED              }
                            { ~~~~~~~~~~              }
                            { TOWARD-GREATER          }
                            { ~~~~~~~~~~~~~~          }
                            { TOWARD-LESSER           }
                            { ~~~~~~~~~~~~~           }
                            { TRUNCATION              }
                              ~~~~~~~~~~

       [ ON SIZE ERROR imperative-statement-1 ]
         ~~~~ ~~~~~

       [ NOT ON SIZE ERROR imperative-statement-2 ]
         ~~~      ~~~~ ~~~~~

  [ END-DIVIDE ]
    ~~~~~~~~~~
```

```
┌─────────────────────────────────────────────────────────────────────┐
│                       DIVIDE INTO GIVING Syntax                        │
└─────────────────────────────────────────────────────────────────────┘

DIVIDE { literal-1    } INTO { literal-2    } GIVING { identifier-3
~~~~~~ { identifier-1 } ~~~~ { identifier-2 } ~~~~~~

              [ ROUNDED [ MODE IS { AWAY-FROM-ZERO          } ] ] }...
                ~~~~~~~    ~~~~    { ~~~~~~~~~~~~~~          }
                                  { NEAREST-AWAY-FROM-ZERO  }
                                  { ~~~~~~~~~~~~~~~~~~~~~~~  }
                                  { NEAREST-EVEN            }
                                  { ~~~~~~~~~~~~            }
                                  { NEAREST-TOWARD-ZERO     }
                                  { ~~~~~~~~~~~~~~~~~~~      }
                                  { PROHIBITED              }
                                  { ~~~~~~~~~~              }
                                  { TOWARD-GREATER          }
                                  { ~~~~~~~~~~~~~~           }
                                  { TOWARD-LESSER           }
                                  { ~~~~~~~~~~~~~            }
                                  { TRUNCATION              }
           [ REMAINDER identifier-4 ]      ~~~~~~~~~~
             ~~~~~~~~~

           [ ON SIZE ERROR imperative-statement-1 ]
             ~~~~ ~~~~~

           [ NOT ON SIZE ERROR imperative-statement-2 ]
             ~~~      ~~~~ ~~~~~

      [ END-DIVIDE ]
        ~~~~~~~~~~
```

```
╭─────────────────────────────────────────────────────────────────────╮
│                        DIVIDE BY GIVING Syntax                        │
╰─────────────────────────────────────────────────────────────────────╯
```

```
DIVIDE { literal-1    } BY { literal-2    } GIVING { identifier-3
~~~~~~ { identifier-1 } ~~ { identifier-2 } ~~~~~~

          [ ROUNDED [ MODE IS { AWAY-FROM-ZERO          } ] ] }...
            ~~~~~~~    ~~~~    { ~~~~~~~~~~~~~~           }
                              { NEAREST-AWAY-FROM-ZERO   }
                              { ~~~~~~~~~~~~~~~~~~~~~~~   }
                              { NEAREST-EVEN             }
                              { ~~~~~~~~~~~~             }
                              { NEAREST-TOWARD-ZERO      }
                              { ~~~~~~~~~~~~~~~~~~~       }
                              { PROHIBITED               }
                              { ~~~~~~~~~~               }
                              { TOWARD-GREATER           }
                              { ~~~~~~~~~~~~~~            }
                              { TOWARD-LESSER            }
                              { ~~~~~~~~~~~~~            }
                              { TRUNCATION               }
                                ~~~~~~~~~~
      [ REMAINDER identifier-4 ]
        ~~~~~~~~~

      [ ON SIZE ERROR imperative-statement-1 ]
        ~~~~ ~~~~~

      [ NOT ON SIZE ERROR imperative-statement-2 ]
        ~~~      ~~~~ ~~~~~

   [ END-DIVIDE ]
     ~~~~~~~~~~
```

```
╭─────────────────────────────────────────────────────────────────────╮
│                             ENTRY Syntax                              │
╰─────────────────────────────────────────────────────────────────────╯
```

```
ENTRY literal-1 [ USING ENTRY-Argument...  ]
~~~~~                 ~~~~~
```

```
╭─────────────────────────────────────────────────────────────────────╮
│                        ENTRY-Argument Syntax                          │
╰─────────────────────────────────────────────────────────────────────╯
```

```
[ BY { REFERENCE } ] identifier-1
     { ~~~~~~~~~ }
     { CONTENT   }
     { ~~~~~~~   }
     { VALUE     }
       ~~~~~
```

```
                            EVALUATE Syntax
```

```
    EVALUATE Selection-Subject-1 [ ALSO Selection-Subject-2 ]...
    ~~~~~~~~                          ~~~~

{ { WHEN Selection-Object-1 [ ALSO Selection-Object-2 ] }...
     ~~~~                     ~~~~

        [ imperative-statement-1 ] }...
  [ WHEN OTHER
    ~~~~ ~~~~~

        imperative-statement-other ]


[ END-EVALUATE ]
  ~~~~~~~~~~~~
```

```
                     EVALUATE Selection Subject Syntax
```

```
{ TRUE        }
{ ~~~~        }
{ FALSE       }
{ ~~~~~       }
{ expression-1 }
{ identifier-1 }
{ literal-1    }
```

```
                     EVALUATE Selection Object Syntax
```

```
{ ANY                                                      }
{ ~~~                                                      }
{ TRUE                                                     }
{ ~~~~                                                     }
{ FALSE                                                    }
{ ~~~~~                                                    }
{ partial-expression-1                                     }
{                                                          }
{ { expression-2 } [ THRU|THROUGH { expression-3 } ] }
{ { identifier-2 }   ~~~~ ~~~~~~~ { identifier-3 }   }
{ { literal-2    }                { literal-3    } }   }
```

```
                             EXIT Syntax
```

```
EXIT [ { PROGRAM            } ]
~~~~   { ~~~~~~~             }
       { FUNCTION            }
       { ~~~~~~~~            }
       { PERFORM [ CYCLE ]   }
       { ~~~~~~~    ~~~~~     }
       { SECTION             }
       { ~~~~~~~             }
       { PARAGRAPH           }
         ~~~~~~~~~
```

```
                             FREE Syntax
```

```
FREE { [ ADDRESS OF ] identifier-1 }...
~~~~     ~~~~~~~
```

```
                           GENERATE Syntax
```

```
GENERATE { report-name-1 }
~~~~~~~~ { identifier-1  }
```

```
                            GOBACK Syntax
```

```
GOBACK
~~~~~~
```

```
                          Simple GO TO Syntax
```

```
GO TO procedure-name-1
~~
```

```
                        GO TO DEPENDING ON Syntax
```

```
GO TO procedure-name-1...
~~

      DEPENDING ON identifier-1
      ~~~~~~~~~
```

IF Syntax

```
IF conditional-expression
~~

THEN { imperative-statement-1 }
     { NEXT SENTENCE           }
       ~~~~ ~~~~~~~~

[ ELSE { imperative-statement-2 } ]
  ~~~~ { NEXT SENTENCE           }
         ~~~~ ~~~~~~~~

[ END-IF ]
  ~~~~~~
```

INITIALIZE Syntax

```
INITIALIZE|INITIALISE identifier-1...
~~~~~~~~~~ ~~~~~~~~~~

    [ WITH FILLER ]
           ~~~~~~

    [ { category-name-1 } TO VALUE ]
      { ALL             }    ~~~~~
        ~~~

    [ THEN REPLACING { category-name-2 DATA BY
           ~~~~~~~~~                        ~~

          [ LENGTH OF ] { literal-1    } }... ]
            ~~~~~~      { identifier-1 }

    [ THEN TO DEFAULT ]
              ~~~~~~~
```

INITIATE Syntax

```
INITIATE report-name-1
~~~~~~~~
```

```
┌─────────────────────────────────────────────────────────────────────┐
│                         INSPECT Syntax                                │
└─────────────────────────────────────────────────────────────────────┘
```

```
INSPECT { literal-1            }
~~~~~~~ { identifier-1         }
        { function-reference-1 }

 [ TALLYING { identifier-2 FOR { ALL|LEADING|TRAILING { literal-2    } }
   ~~~~~~~~                 ~~~ { ~~~ ~~~~~~~ ~~~~~~~~ { identifier-3 } }
                                { CHARACTERS                           }
                                  ~~~~~~~~~~

                [ | { AFTER|BEFORE } INITIAL { literal-3    } | ] }... ]
                  |   ~~~~~ ~~~~~~             { identifier-4 } |

 [ REPLACING { { { ALL|FIRST|LEADING|TRAILING { literal-4    } }
   ~~~~~~~~~   { {   ~~~ ~~~~~ ~~~~~~~ ~~~~~~~~ { identifier-5 } }
              { CHARACTERS                          }
              { ~~~~~~~~~~                          }

             BY { [ ALL ] literal-5 }
             ~~ {   ~~~             }
                { identifier-6      }

                [ | { AFTER|BEFORE } INITIAL { literal-6    } | ] }... ]
                  |   ~~~~~ ~~~~~~             { identifier-7 } |

 [ CONVERTING { { literal-7    } TO { literal-8    }
   ~~~~~~~~~~  { identifier-8 } ~~ { identifier-9 }

                [ | { AFTER|BEFORE } INITIAL { literal-9     } | ] ]
                  |   ~~~~~ ~~~~~~             { identifier-10 } |
```

MERGE Syntax

```
MERGE sort-file-1
~~~~~
     { ON { ASCENDING  } KEY identifier-1...  }...
          { ~~~~~~~~~  }
          { DESCENDING }
            ~~~~~~~~~~

     [ WITH DUPLICATES IN ORDER ]
            ~~~~~~~~~~

     [ COLLATING SEQUENCE IS alphabet-name-1 ]
       ~~~~~~~~~

       USING file-name-1 file-name-2...
       ~~~~~
     { OUTPUT PROCEDURE IS procedure-name-1      }
     { ~~~~~~ ~~~~~~~~~~                          }
     {          [ THRU|THROUGH procedure-name-2 ] }
     {            ~~~~ ~~~~~~~                     }
     { GIVING file-name-3...                      }
     { ~~~~~~                                     }
```

The "DUPLICATES" clause is syntactically recognized but is otherwise non-functional.

Simple MOVE Syntax

```
MOVE { literal-1    } TO identifier-2...
~~~~ { identifier-1 } ~~
```

MOVE CORRESPONDING Syntax

```
MOVE CORRESPONDING identifier-1 TO identifier-2...
~~~~ ~~~~                              ~~
```

```
                          MULTIPLY BY Syntax
```

```
MULTIPLY { literal-1    } BY { identifier-2
~~~~~~~~ { identifier-1 } ~~

        [ ROUNDED [ MODE IS { AWAY-FROM-ZERO          } ] ] }...
          ~~~~~~~    ~~~~   { ~~~~~~~~~~~~~~           }
                           { NEAREST-AWAY-FROM-ZERO   }
                           { ~~~~~~~~~~~~~~~~~~~~~~    }
                           { NEAREST-EVEN             }
                           { ~~~~~~~~~~~~             }
                           { NEAREST-TOWARD-ZERO      }
                           { ~~~~~~~~~~~~~~~~~~~       }
                           { PROHIBITED               }
                           { ~~~~~~~~~~               }
                           { TOWARD-GREATER           }
                           { ~~~~~~~~~~~~~~           }
                           { TOWARD-LESSER            }
                           { ~~~~~~~~~~~~~            }
                           { TRUNCATION               }
                             ~~~~~~~~~~

        [ ON SIZE ERROR imperative-statement-1 ]
          ~~~~ ~~~~~

        [ NOT ON SIZE ERROR imperative-statement-2 ]
          ~~~        ~~~~ ~~~~~

    [ END-DIVIDE ]
      ~~~~~~~~~~
```

```
┌──────────────────────────────────────────────────────────────────┐
│                      MULTIPLY GIVING Syntax                        │
└──────────────────────────────────────────────────────────────────┘
```

```
MULTIPLY { literal-1    } BY { literal-2    } GIVING { identifier-3
~~~~~~~~ { identifier-1 } ~~ { identifier-2 } ~~~~~~

           [ ROUNDED [ MODE IS { AWAY-FROM-ZERO          } ] ] }...
             ~~~~~~~   ~~~~    { ~~~~~~~~~~~~~~          }
                               { NEAREST-AWAY-FROM-ZERO }
                               { ~~~~~~~~~~~~~~~~~~~~~~~ }
                               { NEAREST-EVEN            }
                               { ~~~~~~~~~~~~            }
                               { NEAREST-TOWARD-ZERO     }
                               { ~~~~~~~~~~~~~~~~~~~      }
                               { PROHIBITED              }
                               { ~~~~~~~~~~              }
                               { TOWARD-GREATER          }
                               { ~~~~~~~~~~~~~~           }
                               { TOWARD-LESSER           }
                               { ~~~~~~~~~~~~~            }
                               { TRUNCATION              }
                                 ~~~~~~~~~~

           [ ON SIZE ERROR imperative-statement-1 ]
             ~~~~ ~~~~~

           [ NOT ON SIZE ERROR imperative-statement-2 ]
             ~~~      ~~~~ ~~~~~

     [ END-DIVIDE ]
       ~~~~~~~~~~
```

```
┌──────────────────────────────────────────────────────────────────┐
│                           OPEN Syntax                              │
└──────────────────────────────────────────────────────────────────┘
```

```
OPEN { { INPUT  } [ SHARING WITH { ALL OTHER } ] file-name-1
~~~~ { ~~~~~  }   ~~~~~~~       { ~~~       }
     { OUTPUT }                 { NO OTHER  }
     { ~~~~~~ }                 { ~~        }
     { I-O    }                 { READ ONLY }
     { ~~~    }                   ~~~~ ~~~~
     { EXTEND }
       ~~~~~~

     [ { REVERSED           } ] }...
       { ~~~~~~~~           }
       { WITH { NO REWIND } }
       {      { ~~ ~~~~~~ } }
       {      { LOCK      } }
                ~~~~
```

The "NO REWIND", and "REVERSED" clauses are syntactically recognized but are otherwise
non-functional.

```
┌──────────────────────────────────────────────────────────────────────────┐
│                        Procedural PERFORM Syntax                           │
└──────────────────────────────────────────────────────────────────────────┘
```

```
PERFORM procedure-name-1 [ THRU|THROUGH procedure-name-2 ]
~~~~~~~                    ~~~~ ~~~~~~~

    [ { [ WITH TEST { BEFORE } ] { VARYING-Clause                 } } ]
      {        ~~~~ { ~~~~~~ }   { UNTIL conditional-expression-1 } }
      {              { AFTER  }   ~~~~~                             }
      {               ~~~~~                                        }
      { UNTIL EXIT|FOREVER                                         }
      { ~~~~~ ~~~~ ~~~~~~~                                         }
      { { literal-1    } TIMES                                     }
      { { identifier-1 } ~~~~~                                     }
```

```
┌──────────────────────────────────────────────────────────────────────────┐
│                          Inline PERFORM Syntax                             │
└──────────────────────────────────────────────────────────────────────────┘
```

```
  PERFORM
  ~~~~~~~

    [ { [ WITH TEST { BEFORE } ] { VARYING-Clause                 } } ]
      {        ~~~~ { ~~~~~~ }   { UNTIL conditional-expression-1 } }
      {              { AFTER  }   ~~~~~                             }
      {               ~~~~~                                        }
      { UNTIL EXIT|FOREVER                                         }
      { ~~~~~ ~~~~ ~~~~~~~                                         }
      { { literal-1    } TIMES                                     }
      { { identifier-1 } ~~~~~                                     }

    imperative-statement-1

[ END-PERFORM ]
  ~~~~~~~~~~~
```

```
┌──────────────────────────────────────────────────────────────────────────┐
│                            VARYING Syntax                                  │
└──────────────────────────────────────────────────────────────────────────┘
```

```
VARYING identifier-2 FROM { literal-2    } [ BY { literal-3    } ]
~~~~~~~                    ~~~~ { identifier-3 }   ~~ { identifier-4 }
        [ UNTIL conditional-expression-1 ]
          ~~~~~

[ AFTER identifier-5 FROM { literal-4    } [ BY { literal-5    } ]
  ~~~~~                    ~~~~ { identifier-6 }   ~~ { identifier-7 }
        [ UNTIL conditional-expression-2 ] ]...
          ~~~~~
```

Sequential READ Syntax

```
READ file-name-1 [ { NEXT|PREVIOUS } ] RECORD [ INTO identifier-1 ]
~~~~                { ~~~~ ~~~~~~~~ }                ~~~~
    [ { IGNORING LOCK    } ]
      { ~~~~~~~~ ~~~~     }
      { WITH [ NO ] LOCK }
      {        ~~    ~~~~ }
      { WITH KEPT LOCK    }
      {      ~~~~ ~~~~    }
      { WITH IGNORE LOCK }
      {      ~~~~~~ ~~~~ }
      { WITH WAIT        }
             ~~~~

    [ AT END imperative-statement-1 ]
         ~~~

    [ NOT AT END imperative-statement-2 ]
      ~~~    ~~~

[ END-READ ]
  ~~~~~~~~
```

Random READ Syntax

```
READ file-name-1 RECORD [ INTO identifier-1 ]
~~~~                       ~~~~
    [ { IGNORING LOCK    } ]
      { ~~~~~~~~ ~~~~     }
      { WITH [ NO ] LOCK }
      {        ~~    ~~~~ }
      { WITH KEPT LOCK    }
      {      ~~~~ ~~~~    }
      { WITH IGNORE LOCK }
      {      ~~~~~~ ~~~~ }
      { WITH WAIT        }
             ~~~~

    [ KEY IS identifier-2 ]
      ~~~

    [ INVALID KEY imperative-statement-1 ]
      ~~~~~~~

    [ NOT INVALID KEY imperative-statement-2 ]
      ~~~ ~~~~~~~

[ END-READ ]
  ~~~~~~~~
```

```
                        READY TRACE Syntax
```

```
READY TRACE
~~~~~ ~~~~~
```

```
                          RELEASE Syntax
```

```
RELEASE record-name-1 [ FROM { literal-1    } ]
~~~~~~~                 ~~~~ { identifier-1 }
```

```
                        RESET TRACE Syntax
```

```
RESET TRACE
~~~~~ ~~~~~
```

```
                          RETURN Syntax
```

```
    RETURN sort-file-name-1 RECORD
    ~~~~~~

      [ INTO identifier-1 ]
        ~~~~

        AT END imperative-statement-1
           ~~~

      [ NOT AT END imperative-statement-2 ]
        ~~~    ~~~

  [ END-RETURN ]
    ~~~~~~~~~~
```

```
                          REWRITE Syntax
```

```
    REWRITE record-name-1
    ~~~~~~~

        [ FROM { literal-1    } ]
          ~~~~ { identifier-1 }

        [ WITH [ NO ] LOCK ]
                 ~~    ~~~~

        [ INVALID KEY imperative-statement-1 ]
          ~~~~~~~

        [ NOT INVALID KEY imperative-statement-2 ]
          ~~~ ~~~~~~~

  [ END-REWRITE ]
    ~~~~~~~~~~~
```

ROLLBACK Syntax

```
ROLLBACK
~~~~~~~~
```

SEARCH Syntax

```
   SEARCH table-name-1
   ~~~~~~
       [ VARYING index-name-1 ]
         ~~~~~~~
       [ AT END imperative-statement-1 ]
         ~~~
       { WHEN conditional-expression-1 imperative-statement-2 }...
         ~~~~
[ END-SEARCH ]
  ~~~~~~~~~~
```

SEARCH ALL Syntax

```
   SEARCH ALL table-name-1
   ~~~~~~ ~~~
       [ AT END imperative-statement-1 ]
         ~~~
         WHEN conditional-expression-1 imperative-statement-2
         ~~~~
[ END-SEARCH ]
  ~~~~~~~~~~
```

SET ENVIRONMENT Syntax

```
SET ENVIRONMENT { literal-1    } TO { literal-2    }
~~~ ~~~~~~~~~~~ { identifier-1 } ~~ { identifier-2 }
```

SET Program-Pointer Syntax

```
SET program-pointer-1 TO ENTRY { literal-1    }
~~~                   ~~ ~~~~~ { identifier-1 }
```

SET ADDRESS Syntax

```
SET [ ADDRESS OF ] { pointer-name-1 }...
~~~   ~~~~~~~ ~~    { identifier-1   }

    TO [ ADDRESS OF ]  { pointer-name-2 }
    ~~   ~~~~~~~ ~~     { identifier-2   }
```

```
┌──────────────────────────────────────────────────────────────────────┐
│                          SET Index Syntax                              │
└──────────────────────────────────────────────────────────────────────┘

SET index-name-1 TO { literal-1    }
~~~              ~~ { identifier-2 }
```

```
┌──────────────────────────────────────────────────────────────────────┐
│                         SET UP/DOWN Syntax                             │
└──────────────────────────────────────────────────────────────────────┘

SET identifier-1 { UP   } BY [ LENGTH OF ] { literal-1    }
~~~              { ~~   } ~~   ~~~~~~ ~~   { identifier-2 }
                 { DOWN }
                   ~~~~
```

```
┌──────────────────────────────────────────────────────────────────────┐
│                       SET Condition Name Syntax                        │
└──────────────────────────────────────────────────────────────────────┘

SET condition-name-1...  TO { TRUE  }
~~~                      ~~ { ~~~~  }
                            { FALSE }
                              ~~~~~
```

```
┌──────────────────────────────────────────────────────────────────────┐
│                          SET Switch Syntax                             │
└──────────────────────────────────────────────────────────────────────┘

SET mnemonic-name-1...  TO { ON  }
~~~                     ~~ { ~~  }
                           { OFF }
                             ~~~
```

```
┌──────────────────────────────────────────────────────────────────────┐
│                         SET ATTRIBUTE Syntax                           │
└──────────────────────────────────────────────────────────────────────┘

SET identifier-1 ATTRIBUTE { { BELL          } { ON  }...
~~~              ~~~~~~~~~  { { ~~~~          } { ~~  }
                             { BLINK         } { OFF }
                             { ~~~~~         }   ~~~
                             { HIGHLIGHT     }
                             { ~~~~~~~~~     }
                             { LEFTLINE      }
                             { ~~~~~~~~      }
                             { LOWLIGHT      }
                             { ~~~~~~~~      }
                             { OVERLINE      }
                             { ~~~~~~~~      }
                             { REVERSE-VIDEO }
                             { ~~~~~~~~~~~~~ }
                             { UNDERLINE     }
                               ~~~~~~~~~
```

```
┌──────────────────────────────────────────────────────────────────────────┐
│                          File-Based SORT Syntax                            │
└──────────────────────────────────────────────────────────────────────────┘
```

```
SORT sort-file-1
~~~~

    { ON { ASCENDING  } KEY identifier-1... }...
         { ~~~~~~~~~  }
         { DESCENDING }
           ~~~~~~~~~~

    [ WITH DUPLICATES IN ORDER ]
           ~~~~~~~~~~

    [ COLLATING SEQUENCE IS alphabet-name-1 ]
      ~~~~~~~~~


    { INPUT PROCEDURE IS procedure-name-1        }
    { ~~~~~ ~~~~~~~~~                             }
    {         [ THRU|THROUGH procedure-name-2 ]  }
    {           ~~~~ ~~~~~~~                      }
    { USING file-name-1 ...                       }
      ~~~~~


    { OUTPUT PROCEDURE IS procedure-name-3       }
    { ~~~~~~ ~~~~~~~~~                            }
    {         [ THRU|THROUGH procedure-name-4 ]  }
    {           ~~~~ ~~~~~~~                      }
    { GIVING  file-name-3 ...                     }
      ~~~~~~
```

The "DUPLICATES" clause is syntactically recognized but is otherwise non-functional.

```
┌──────────────────────────────────────────────────────────────────────────┐
│                            Table SORT Syntax                               │
└──────────────────────────────────────────────────────────────────────────┘
```

```
SORT table-name-1
~~~~

    { ON { ASCENDING  } KEY identifier-1... }...
         { ~~~~~~~~~  }
         { DESCENDING }
           ~~~~~~~~~~

    [ WITH DUPLICATES IN ORDER ]
           ~~~~~~~~~~

    [ COLLATING SEQUENCE IS alphabet-name-1 ]
      ~~~~~~~~~
```

The "DUPLICATES" clause is syntactically recognized but is otherwise non-functional.

```
                              START Syntax
```

```
    START file-name-1
    ~~~~~
        [ { FIRST                                              } ]
          { ~~~~~                                              }
          { LAST                                               }
          { ~~~~                                               }
          { KEY { IS EQUAL TO | IS = | EQUALS        } identifier-1 }
                {    ~~~~~             ~~~~~~         }
                { IS GREATER THAN | IS >             }
                {    ~~~~~~~                          }
                { IS GREATER THAN OR EQUAL TO | IS >= }
                {    ~~~~~~~          ~~ ~~~~~        }
                { IS NOT LESS THAN                    }
                {    ~~~ ~~~~                          }
                { IS LESS THAN | IS <                 }
                {    ~~~~                              }
                { IS LESS THAN OR EQUAL TO | IS <=    }
                {    ~~~~          ~~ ~~~~~           }
                { IS NOT GREATER THAN                 }
                     ~~~ ~~~~~~~

        [ INVALID KEY imperative-statement-1 ]
          ~~~~~~~

        [ NOT INVALID KEY imperative-statement-2 ]
          ~~~ ~~~~~~~

    [ END-START ]
      ~~~~~~~~~
```

```
                              STOP Syntax
```

```
    STOP { RUN [ { RETURNING|GIVING { literal-1    }        } ] }
    ~~~~ { ~~~   { ~~~~~~~~~ ~~~~~~ { identifier-1 }        }   }
         {       {                                         }   }
         {       { WITH { ERROR  } STATUS [ { literal-2    } ] } }
         {       {      { ~~~~~  }           { identifier-2 }   } }
         {       {      { NORMAL }                         }   }
         {              ~~~~~~                              }
         { literal-3                                        }
```

```
                          STRING Syntax
```

```
STRING
~~~~~~

    { { literal-1    } [ DELIMITED BY { SIZE          } ] }...
      { identifier-1 }   ~~~~~~~~~~~   { ~~~~          }
                                      { literal-2     }
      INTO identifier-3               { identifier-2  }
      ~~~~

    [ WITH POINTER identifier-4 ]
           ~~~~~~~

    [ ON OVERFLOW imperative-statement-1 ]
         ~~~~~~~~

    [ NOT ON OVERFLOW imperative-statement-2 ]
      ~~~     ~~~~~~~~

[ END-STRING ]
  ~~~~~~~~~~
```

```
                       SUBTRACT FROM Syntax
```

```
SUBTRACT { literal-1    }...   FROM { identifier-2
~~~~~~~~ { identifier-1 }      ~~~~

         [ ROUNDED [ MODE IS { AWAY-FROM-ZERO          } ] ] }...
           ~~~~~~~    ~~~~    { ~~~~~~~~~~~~~~          }
                             { NEAREST-AWAY-FROM-ZERO  }
                             { ~~~~~~~~~~~~~~~~~~~~~~~  }
                             { NEAREST-EVEN            }
                             { ~~~~~~~~~~~~~          }
                             { NEAREST-TOWARD-ZERO     }
                             { ~~~~~~~~~~~~~~~~~~~     }
                             { PROHIBITED              }
                             { ~~~~~~~~~~              }
                             { TOWARD-GREATER          }
                             { ~~~~~~~~~~~~~~          }
                             { TOWARD-LESSER           }
                             { ~~~~~~~~~~~~~           }
                             { TRUNCATION              }
                               ~~~~~~~~~~

    [ ON SIZE ERROR imperative-statement-1 ]
         ~~~~ ~~~~~

    [ NOT ON SIZE ERROR imperative-statement-2 ]
      ~~~     ~~~~ ~~~~~

[ END-SUBTRACT ]
  ~~~~~~~~~~~~
```

```
┌──────────────────────────────────────────────────────────────────────────┐
│                          SUBTRACT GIVING Syntax                            │
└──────────────────────────────────────────────────────────────────────────┘

     SUBTRACT { literal-1    }...  FROM identifier-2
     ~~~~~~~~ { identifier-1 }     ~~~~

         GIVING { identifier-3
         ~~~~~~

             [ ROUNDED [ MODE IS { AWAY-FROM-ZERO          } ] ] }...
               ~~~~~~~   ~~~~    { ~~~~~~~~~~~~~            }
                                 { NEAREST-AWAY-FROM-ZERO  }
                                 { ~~~~~~~~~~~~~~~~~~~~~~~  }
                                 { NEAREST-EVEN            }
                                 { ~~~~~~~~~~~~            }
                                 { NEAREST-TOWARD-ZERO     }
                                 { ~~~~~~~~~~~~~~~~~~~      }
                                 { PROHIBITED              }
                                 { ~~~~~~~~~~              }
                                 { TOWARD-GREATER          }
                                 { ~~~~~~~~~~~~~~           }
                                 { TOWARD-LESSER           }
                                 { ~~~~~~~~~~~~~           }
                                 { TRUNCATION              }
                                   ~~~~~~~~~~

         [ ON SIZE ERROR imperative-statement-1 ]
           ~~~~ ~~~~~

         [ NOT ON SIZE ERROR imperative-statement-2 ]
           ~~~     ~~~~ ~~~~~

     [ END-SUBTRACT ]
       ~~~~~~~~~~~~
```

SUBTRACT CORRESPONDING Syntax

```
SUBTRACT CORRESPONDING identifier-1 FROM identifier-2
~~~~~~~~                          ~~~~

     [ ROUNDED [ MODE IS { AWAY-FROM-ZERO         } ] ]
       ~~~~~~~   ~~~~     { ~~~~~~~~~~~~~~         }
                         { NEAREST-AWAY-FROM-ZERO }
                         { ~~~~~~~~~~~~~~~~~~~~~~~ }
                         { NEAREST-EVEN           }
                         { ~~~~~~~~~~~~           }
                         { NEAREST-TOWARD-ZERO    }
                         { ~~~~~~~~~~~~~~~~~~~     }
                         { PROHIBITED             }
                         { ~~~~~~~~~~             }
                         { TOWARD-GREATER         }
                         { ~~~~~~~~~~~~~~         }
                         { TOWARD-LESSER          }
                         { ~~~~~~~~~~~~~          }
                         { TRUNCATION             }
                           ~~~~~~~~~~

     [ ON SIZE ERROR imperative-statement-1 ]
         ~~~~ ~~~~~

     [ NOT ON SIZE ERROR imperative-statement-2 ]
       ~~~      ~~~~ ~~~~~

 [ END-SUBTRACT ]
   ~~~~~~~~~~~~
```

SUPPRESS Syntax

```
SUPPRESS PRINTING
~~~~~~~~
```

TERMINATE Syntax

```
TERMINATE report-name-1...
~~~~~~~~~
```

TRANSFORM Syntax

```
TRANSFORM identifier-1 FROM { literal-1    } TO { literal-2    }
~~~~~~~~~              ~~~~ { identifier-2 } ~~ { identifier-3 }
```

UNLOCK Syntax

```
UNLOCK filename-1 RECORD|RECORDS
~~~~~~
```

UNSTRING Syntax

```
    UNSTRING identifier-1
    ~~~~~~~~

         DELIMITED BY { [ ALL ] literal-1 } [ OR { [ ALL ] literal-2 } ]...
         ~~~~~~~~~    {    ~~~            }  ~~ {    ~~~            }
                      { identifier-2      }      { identifier-3       }

         INTO { identifier-4
         ~~~~ [ DELIMITER IN identifier-5 ] [ COUNT IN identifier-6 ] }...
              ~~~~~~~~~                        ~~~~~

         [ WITH POINTER identifier-7 ]
                ~~~~~~~

         [ TALLYING IN identifier-8 ]
           ~~~~~~~~

         [ ON OVERFLOW imperative-statement-1 ]
              ~~~~~~~~

         [ NOT ON OVERFLOW imperative-statement-2 ]
           ~~~      ~~~~~~~~

    [ END-UNSTRING ]
      ~~~~~~~~~~~~
```

WRITE Syntax

```
    WRITE record-name-1
    ~~~~~

         [ FROM { literal-1    } ]
           ~~~~ { identifier-1 }

         [ WITH [ NO ] LOCK ]
                  ~~   ~~~~

         [ { BEFORE } ADVANCING { { literal-2    } LINE|LINES } ]
           { ~~~~~~ }           { { identifier-2            }
           { AFTER  }           { PAGE                      }
             ~~~~~             { ~~~~                       }
                                { mnemonic-name-1            }

         [ AT END-OF-PAGE|EOP imperative-statement-1 ]
              ~~~~~~~~~~~ ~~~

         [ NOT AT END-OF-PAGE|EOP imperative-statement-2 ]
           ~~~     ~~~~~~~~~~~ ~~~

         [ INVALID KEY imperative-statement-3 ]
           ~~~~~~~

         [ NOT INVALID KEY imperative-statement-4 ]
           ~~~ ~~~~~~~

    [ END-WRITE ]
      ~~~~~~~~~
```

6. Intrinsic Functions Syntax

ABS Function Syntax

ABS(number)
~~~

ACOS Function Syntax

ACOS(cosine)
~~~~

ANNUITY Function Syntax

ANNUITY(interest-rate, number-of-periods)
~~~~~~~

ASIN Function Syntax

ASIN(sine)
~~~~

ATAN Function Syntax

ATAN(tangent)
~~~~

BYTE-LENGTH Function Syntax

BYTE-LENGTH(string)
~~~~~~~~~~~

CHAR Function Syntax

CHAR(integer)
~~~~

COMBINED-DATETIME Function Syntax

COMBINED-DATETIME(days, seconds)
~~~~~~~~~~~~~~~~~

CONCATENATE Function Syntax

```
CONCATENATE(string-1 [, string-2 ]...)
~~~~~~~~~~~
```

COS Function Syntax

```
COS(angle)
~~~
```

CURRENCY-SYMBOL Function Syntax

```
CURRENCY-SYMBOL
~~~~~~~~~~~~~~~
```

CURRENT-DATE Function Syntax

```
CURRENT-DATE
~~~~~~~~~~~~
```

DATE-OF-INTEGER Function Syntax

```
DATE-OF-INTEGER(integer)
~~~~~~~~~~~~~~~
```

DATE-TO-YYYYMMDD Function Syntax

```
DATE-TO-YYYYMMDD(yymmdd [, yy-cutoff ])
~~~~~~~~~~~~~~~~
```

DAY-OF-INTEGER Function Syntax

```
DAY-OF-INTEGER(integer)
~~~~~~~~~~~~~~
```

DAY-TO-YYYYDDD Function Syntax

```
DAY-TO-YYYYDDD(yyddd [, yy-cutoff])
~~~~~~~~~~~~~~
```

E Function Syntax

```
E
~
```

EXCEPTION-FILE Function Syntax

```
EXCEPTION-FILE
~~~~~~~~~~~~~~
```

EXCEPTION-LOCATION Function Syntax

```
EXCEPTION-LOCATION
~~~~~~~~~~~~~~~~~~
```

EXCEPTION-STATEMENT Function Syntax

```
EXCEPTION-STATEMENT
~~~~~~~~~~~~~~~~~~~
```

EXCEPTION-STATUS Function Syntax

```
EXCEPTION-STATUS
~~~~~~~~~~~~~~~~
```

EXP Function Syntax

```
EXP(number)
~~~
```

EXP10 Function Syntax

```
EXP10(number)
~~~~~
```

FACTORIAL Function Syntax

```
FACTORIAL(number)
~~~~~~~~~
```

FRACTION-PART Function Syntax

```
FRACTION-PART(number)
~~~~~~~~~~~~~
```

HIGHEST-ALGEBRAIC Function Syntax

```
HIGHEST-ALGEBRAIC(numeric-identifier)
~~~~~~~~~~~~~~~~~
```

INTEGER Function Syntax

```
INTEGER(number)
~~~~~~~
```

INTEGER-OF-DATE Function Syntax

```
INTEGER-OF-DATE(date)
~~~~~~~~~~~~~~~
```

INTEGER-OF-DAY Function Syntax

```
INTEGER-OF-DAY(date)
~~~~~~~~~~~~~~
```

INTEGER-PART Function Syntax

```
INTEGER-PART(number)
~~~~~~~~~~~~
```

LENGTH Function Syntax

```
LENGTH(string)
~~~~~~
```

LENGTH-AN Function Syntax

```
LENGTH-AN(string)
~~~~~~~~~
```

LOCALE-COMPARE Function Syntax

```
LOCALE-COMPARE(argument-1, argument-2 [ , locale ])
~~~~~~~~~~~~~~
```

LOCALE-DATE Function Syntax

```
LOCALE-DATE(date [, locale ])
~~~~~~~~~~~
```

LOCALE-TIME Function Syntax

```
LOCALE-TIME(time [, locale ])
~~~~~~~~~~~
```

LOCALE-TIME-FROM-SECONDS Function Syntax

```
LOCALE-TIME-FROM-SECONDS(seconds [, locale ])
~~~~~~~~~~~~~~~~~~~~~~~~
```

LOG Function Syntax

```
LOG(number)
~~~
```

LOG10 Function Syntax

```
LOG10(number)
~~~~~
```

LOWER-CASE Function Syntax

```
LOWER-CASE(string)
~~~~~~~~~~
```

LOWEST-ALGEBRAIC Function Syntax

```
LOWEST-ALGEBRAIC(numeric-identifier)
~~~~~~~~~~~~~~~~
```

MAX Function Syntax

```
MAX(number-1 [, number-2 ]...)
~~~
```

MEAN Function Syntax

```
MEAN(number-1 [, number-2 ]...)
~~~~
```

MEDIAN Function Syntax

```
MEDIAN(number-1 [, number-2 ]...)
~~~~~~
```

MIDRANGE Function Syntax

```
MIDRANGE(number-1 [, number-2 ]...)
~~~~~~~~
```

MIN Function Syntax

```
MIN(number-1 [, number-2 ]...)
~~~
```

MOD Function Syntax

```
MOD(value, modulus)
~~~
```

MODULE-CALLER-ID Function Syntax

```
MODULE-CALLER-ID
~~~~~~~~~~~~~~~~
```

MODULE-DATE Function Syntax

```
MODULE-DATE
~~~~~~~~~~~
```

MODULE-FORMATTED-DATE Function Syntax

```
MODULE-FORMATTED-DATE
~~~~~~~~~~~~~~~~~~~~~
```

MODULE-ID Function Syntax

```
MODULE-ID
~~~~~~~~~
```

MODULE-PATH Function Syntax

```
MODULE-PATH
~~~~~~~~~~~
```

MODULE-SOURCE Function Syntax

```
MODULE-SOURCE
~~~~~~~~~~~~~
```

MODULE-TIME Function Syntax

```
MODULE-TIME
~~~~~~~~~~~
```

MONETARY-DECIMAL-POINT Function Syntax

```
MONETARY-DECIMAL-POINT
~~~~~~~~~~~~~~~~~~~~~~~
```

MONETARY-THOUSANDS-SEPARATOR Function Syntax

```
MONETARY-THOUSANDS-SEPARATOR
~~~~~~~~~~~~~~~~~~~~~~~~~~~~~
```

NUMERIC-DECIMAL-POINT Function Syntax

```
NUMERIC-DECIMAL-POINT
~~~~~~~~~~~~~~~~~~~~~
```

NUMERIC-THOUSANDS-SEPARATOR Function Syntax

```
NUMERIC-THOUSANDS-SEPARATOR
~~~~~~~~~~~~~~~~~~~~~~~~~~~~
```

NUMVAL Function Syntax

```
NUMVAL(string)
~~~~~~
```

NUMVAL-C Function Syntax

```
NUMVAL-C(string[,symbol])
~~~~~~~~
```

NUMVAL-F Function Syntax

```
NUMVAL-F(char)
~~~~~~~~
```

ORD Function Syntax

```
ORD(char)
~~~
```

ORD-MAX Function Syntax

```
ORD-MAX(char-1 [, char-2 ]...)
~~~~~~~
```

ORD-MIN Function Syntax

```
ORD-MIN(char-1 [, char-2 ]...)
~~~~~~~
```

PI Function Syntax

```
PI
~~
```

PRESENT-VALUE Function Syntax

```
PRESENT-VALUE(rate, value-1 [, value-2 ])
~~~~~~~~~~~~~
```

RANDOM Function Syntax

```
RANDOM[(seed)]
~~~~~~
```

RANGE Function Syntax

```
RANGE(number-1 [, number-2 ]...)
~~~~~
```

REM Function Syntax

```
REM(number,divisor)
~~~
```

REVERSE Function Syntax

```
REVERSE(string)
~~~~~~~
```

SECONDS-FROM-FORMATTED-TIME Function Syntax

```
SECONDS-FROM-FORMATTED-TIME(format,time)
~~~~~~~~~~~~~~~~~~~~~~~~~~~
```

SECONDS-PAST-MIDNIGHT Function Syntax

```
SECONDS-PAST-MIDNIGHT
~~~~~~~~~~~~~~~~~~~~~
```

SIGN Function Syntax

```
SIGN(number)
~~~~
```

SIN Function Syntax

```
SIN(angle)
~~~
```

SQRT Function Syntax

```
SQRT(number)
~~~~
```

STANDARD-DEVIATION Function Syntax

```
STANDARD-DEVIATION(number-1 [, number-2 ]...)
~~~~~~~~~~~~~~~~~~
```

STORED-CHAR-LENGTH Function Syntax

```
STORED-CHAR-LENGTH(string)
~~~~~~~~~~~~~~~~~~
```

SUBSTITUTE Function Syntax

```
SUBSTITUTE(string, from-1, to-1 [, from-n, to-n ]...)
~~~~~~~~~~
```

SUBSTITUTE-CASE Function Syntax

```
SUBSTITUTE-CASE(string, from-1, to-1 [, from-n, to-n ]...)
~~~~~~~~~~~~~~~
```

SUM Function Syntax

```
SUM(number-1 [, number-2 ]...)
~~~
```

TAN Function Syntax

```
TAN(angle)
~~~
```

TEST-DATE-YYYYMMDD Function Syntax

```
TEST-DATE-YYYYMMDD(date)
~~~~~~~~~~~~~~~~~~
```

TEST-DAY-YYYYDDD Function Syntax

```
TEST-DATE-YYYYDDD(date)
~~~~~~~~~~~~~~~~~
```

TEST-NUMVAL Function Syntax

```
TEST-NUMVAL(string)
~~~~~~~~~~~
```

TEST-NUMVAL-C Function Syntax

```
TEST-NUMVAL-C(string[,symbol])
~~~~~~~~~~~~~
```

TEST-NUMVAL-F Function Syntax

```
TEST-NUMVAL-F(string)
~~~~~~~~~~~~~
```

TRIM Function Syntax

```
TRIM(string [, LEADING|TRAILING ])
~~~~          ~~~~~~~ ~~~~~~~~
```

UPPER-CASE Function Syntax

```
UPPER-CASE(string)
~~~~~~~~~~
```

VARIANCE Function Syntax

```
VARIANCE(number-1 [, number-2 ]...)
~~~~~~~~
```

WHEN-COMPILED Function Syntax

```
WHEN-COMPILED
~~~~~~~~~~~~~
```

YEAR-TO-YYYY Function Syntax

```
YEAR-TO-YYYY(yy [, yy-cutoff ])
~~~~~~~~~~~~
```

7. Built-In Subroutines Syntax

C$CALLEDBY Built-In Subroutine Syntax

```
CALL "C$CALLEDBY" USING prog-name-area
     ~~~~          ~~~~~
```

C$CHDIR Built-In Subroutine Syntax

```
CALL "C$CHDIR" USING directory-path, result
     ~~~~       ~~~~~
```

C$COPY Built-In Subroutine Syntax

```
CALL "C$COPY" USING src-file-path, dest-file-path, 0
     ~~~~      ~~~~~
```

C$DELETE Built-In Subroutine Syntax

```
CALL "C$DELETE" USING file-path, 0
     ~~~~        ~~~~~
```

C$FILEINFO Built-In Subroutine Syntax

```
CALL "C$FILEINFO" USING file-path, file-info
     ~~~~          ~~~~~
```

C$GETPID Built-In Subroutine Syntax

```
CALL "C$GETPID"
     ~~~~
```

C$JUSTIFY Built-In Subroutine Syntax

```
CALL "C$JUSTIFY" USING data-item, "justification-type"
     ~~~~         ~~~~~
```

C$MAKEDIR Built-In Subroutine Syntax

```
CALL "C$MAKEDIR" USING dir-path
     ~~~~         ~~~~~
```

```
                          C$NARG Built-In Subroutine Syntax
```

```
CALL "C$NARG" USING arg-count-result
~~~~          ~~~~~
```

```
                        C$PARAMSIZE Built-In Subroutine Syntax
```

```
CALL "C$PARAMSIZE" USING argument-number
~~~~               ~~~~~
```

```
                        C$PRINTABLE Built-In Subroutine Syntax
```

```
CALL "C$PRINTABLE" USING data-item [ , char ]
~~~~               ~~~~~
```

```
                          C$SLEEP Built-In Subroutine Syntax
```

```
CALL "C$SLEEP" USING seconds-to-sleep
~~~~           ~~~~~
```

```
                         C$TOLOWER Built-In Subroutine Syntax
```

```
CALL "C$TOLOWER" USING data-item, BY VALUE convert-length
~~~~             ~~~~~             ~~~~~
```

```
                         C$TOUPPER Built-In Subroutine Syntax
```

```
CALL "C$TOUPPER" USING data-item, BY VALUE convert-length
~~~~             ~~~~~             ~~~~~
```

```
                           CBL_AND Built-In Subroutine Syntax
```

```
CALL "CBL_AND" USING item-1, item-2, BY VALUE byte-length
~~~~           ~~~~~                  ~~~~~
```

```
                       CBL_CHANGE_DIR Built-In Subroutine Syntax
```

```
CALL "CBL_CHANGE_DIR" USING directory-path
~~~~                  ~~~~~
```

```
                     CBL_CHECK_FILE_EXIST Built-In Subroutine Syntax
```

```
CALL "CBL_CHECK_FILE_EXIST" USING file-path, file-info
~~~~                        ~~~~~
```

CBL_CLOSE_FILE Built-In Subroutine Syntax

```
CALL "CBL_CLOSE_FILE" USING file-handle
~~~~                   ~~~~~
```

CBL_COPY_FILE Built-In Subroutine Syntax

```
CALL "CBL_COPY_FILE" USING src-file-path, dest-file-path
~~~~                 ~~~~~
```

CBL_CREATE_DIR Built-In Subroutine Syntax

```
CALL "CBL_CREATE_DIR" USING dir-path
~~~~                  ~~~~~
```

CBL_CREATE_FILE Built-In Subroutine Syntax

```
CALL "CBL_CREATE_FILE" USING file-path, 2, 0, 0, file-handle
~~~~                   ~~~~~
```

CBL_DELETE_DIR Built-In Subroutine Syntax

```
CALL "CBL_DELETE_DIR" USING dir-path
~~~~                  ~~~~~
```

CBL_DELETE_FILE Built-In Subroutine Syntax

```
CALL "CBL_DELETE_FILE" USING file-path
~~~~                   ~~~~~
```

CBL_EQ Built-In Subroutine Syntax

```
CALL "CBL_EQ" USING item-1, item-2, BY VALUE byte-length
~~~~          ~~~~~                          ~~~~~
```

CBL_ERROR_PROC Built-In Subroutine Syntax

```
CALL "CBL_ERROR_PROC" USING function, program-pointer
~~~~                  ~~~~~
```

CBL_EXIT_PROC Built-In Subroutine Syntax

```
CALL "CBL_EXIT_PROC" USING function, program-pointer
~~~~                 ~~~~~
```

CBL_FLUSH_FILE Built-In Subroutine Syntax

```
CALL "CBL_FLUSH_FILE" USING file-handle
~~~~                        ~~~~~
```

CBL_GET_CSR_POS Built-In Subroutine Syntax

```
CALL "CBL_GET_CSR_POS" USING cursor-locn-buffer
~~~~                         ~~~~~
```

CBL_GET_CURRENT_DIR Built-In Subroutine Syntax

```
CALL "CBL_GET_CURRENT_DIR" USING BY VALUE 0,
~~~~                             ~~~~~    ~~~~~

                                 BY VALUE length,
                                    ~~~~~

                                 BY REFERENCE buffer
                                    ~~~~~~~~~~
```

CBL_GET_SCR_SIZE Built-In Subroutine Syntax

```
CALL "CBL_GET_SCR_SIZE" USING no-of-lines, no-of-cols
~~~~                          ~~~~~
```

CBL_IMP Built-In Subroutine Syntax

```
CALL "CBL_IMP" USING item-1, item-2, BY VALUE byte-length
~~~~                 ~~~~~            ~~~~~
```

CBL_NIMP Built-In Subroutine Syntax

```
CALL "CBL_NIMP" USING item-1, item-2, BY VALUE byte-length
~~~~                  ~~~~~            ~~~~~
```

CBL_NOR Built-In Subroutine Syntax

```
CALL "CBL_NOR" USING item-1, item-2, BY VALUE byte-length
~~~~                 ~~~~~            ~~~~~
```

CBL_NOT Built-In Subroutine Syntax

```
CALL "CBL_NOT" USING item-1, BY VALUE byte-length
~~~~                 ~~~~~   ~~~~~
```

```
                    CBL_OC_NANOSLEEP Built-In Subroutine Syntax

CALL "CBL_OC_NANOSLEEP" USING nanoseconds-to-sleep
~~~~                          ~~~~~


                    CBL_OPEN_FILE Built-In Subroutine Syntax

CALL "CBL_OPEN_FILE" USING file-path, access-mode, 0, 0, handle
~~~~                       ~~~~~


                        CBL_OR Built-In Subroutine Syntax

CALL "CBL_OR" USING item-1, item-2, BY VALUE byte-length
~~~~                ~~~~~              ~~~~~


                    CBL_READ_FILE Built-In Subroutine Syntax

CALL "CBL_READ_FILE" USING handle, offset, nbytes, flag, buffer
~~~~                       ~~~~~


                    CBL_RENAME_FILE Built-In Subroutine Syntax

CALL "CBL_RENAME_FILE" USING old-file-path, new-file-path
~~~~                         ~~~~~


                    CBL_TOLOWER Built-In Subroutine Syntax

CALL "CBL_TOLOWER" USING data-item, BY VALUE convert-length
~~~~                     ~~~~~              ~~~~~


                    CBL_TOUPPER Built-In Subroutine Syntax

CALL "CBL_TOUPPER" USING data-item, BY VALUE convert-length
~~~~                     ~~~~~              ~~~~~


                    CBL_WRITE_FILE Built-In Subroutine Syntax

CALL "CBL_WRITE_FILE" USING handle, offset, nbytes, 0, buffer
~~~~                        ~~~~~


                        CBL_XOR Built-In Subroutine Syntax

CALL "CBL_XOR" USING item-1, item-2, BY VALUE byte-length
~~~~                 ~~~~~              ~~~~~
```

SYSTEM Built-In Subroutine Syntax

```
CALL "SYSTEM" USING command
~~~~          ~~~~~
```

X"91" Built-In Subroutine Syntax

```
CALL X"91" USING return-code, function-code, binary-variable-arg
~~~~       ~~~~~
```

X"E4" Built-In Subroutine Syntax

```
CALL X"E4"
~~~~
```

X"E5" Built-In Subroutine Syntax

```
CALL X"E5"
~~~~
```

X"F4" Built-In Subroutine Syntax

```
CALL X"F4" USING byte, table
~~~~       ~~~~~
```

X"F5" Built-In Subroutine Syntax

```
CALL X"F5" USING byte, table
~~~~       ~~~~~
```

8. GNU Free Documentation License

Version 1.3, 3 November 2008

Copyright © 2000, 2001, 2002, 2007, 2008 Free Software Foundation, Inc.
http://fsf.org/

Everyone is permitted to copy and distribute verbatim copies
of this license document, but changing it is not allowed.

0. PREAMBLE

The purpose of this License is to make a manual, textbook, or other functional and
useful document *free* in the sense of freedom: to assure everyone the effective freedom
to copy and redistribute it, with or without modifying it, either commercially or noncommercially. Secondarily, this License preserves for the author and publisher a way
to get credit for their work, while not being considered responsible for modifications
made by others.

This License is a kind of "copyleft", which means that derivative works of the document
must themselves be free in the same sense. It complements the GNU General Public
License, which is a copyleft license designed for free software.

We have designed this License in order to use it for manuals for free software, because
free software needs free documentation: a free program should come with manuals
providing the same freedoms that the software does. But this License is not limited to
software manuals; it can be used for any textual work, regardless of subject matter or
whether it is published as a printed book. We recommend this License principally for
works whose purpose is instruction or reference.

1. APPLICABILITY AND DEFINITIONS

This License applies to any manual or other work, in any medium, that contains a
notice placed by the copyright holder saying it can be distributed under the terms
of this License. Such a notice grants a world-wide, royalty-free license, unlimited in
duration, to use that work under the conditions stated herein. The "Document",
below, refers to any such manual or work. Any member of the public is a licensee, and
is addressed as "you". You accept the license if you copy, modify or distribute the work
in a way requiring permission under copyright law.

A "Modified Version" of the Document means any work containing the Document or
a portion of it, either copied verbatim, or with modifications and/or translated into
another language.

A "Secondary Section" is a named appendix or a front-matter section of the Document
that deals exclusively with the relationship of the publishers or authors of the Document
to the Document's overall subject (or to related matters) and contains nothing that
could fall directly within that overall subject. (Thus, if the Document is in part a
textbook of mathematics, a Secondary Section may not explain any mathematics.) The
relationship could be a matter of historical connection with the subject or with related
matters, or of legal, commercial, philosophical, ethical or political position regarding
them.

The "Invariant Sections" are certain Secondary Sections whose titles are designated, as being those of Invariant Sections, in the notice that says that the Document is released under this License. If a section does not fit the above definition of Secondary then it is not allowed to be designated as Invariant. The Document may contain zero Invariant Sections. If the Document does not identify any Invariant Sections then there are none.

The "Cover Texts" are certain short passages of text that are listed, as Front-Cover Texts or Back-Cover Texts, in the notice that says that the Document is released under this License. A Front-Cover Text may be at most 5 words, and a Back-Cover Text may be at most 25 words.

A "Transparent" copy of the Document means a machine-readable copy, represented in a format whose specification is available to the general public, that is suitable for revising the document straightforwardly with generic text editors or (for images composed of pixels) generic paint programs or (for drawings) some widely available drawing editor, and that is suitable for input to text formatters or for automatic translation to a variety of formats suitable for input to text formatters. A copy made in an otherwise Transparent file format whose markup, or absence of markup, has been arranged to thwart or discourage subsequent modification by readers is not Transparent. An image format is not Transparent if used for any substantial amount of text. A copy that is not "Transparent" is called "Opaque".

Examples of suitable formats for Transparent copies include plain ASCII without markup, Texinfo input format, LaTeX input format, SGML or XML using a publicly available DTD, and standard-conforming simple HTML, PostScript or PDF designed for human modification. Examples of transparent image formats include PNG, XCF and JPG. Opaque formats include proprietary formats that can be read and edited only by proprietary word processors, SGML or XML for which the DTD and/or processing tools are not generally available, and the machine-generated HTML, PostScript or PDF produced by some word processors for output purposes only.

The "Title Page" means, for a printed book, the title page itself, plus such following pages as are needed to hold, legibly, the material this License requires to appear in the title page. For works in formats which do not have any title page as such, "Title Page" means the text near the most prominent appearance of the work's title, preceding the beginning of the body of the text.

The "publisher" means any person or entity that distributes copies of the Document to the public.

A section "Entitled XYZ" means a named subunit of the Document whose title either is precisely XYZ or contains XYZ in parentheses following text that translates XYZ in another language. (Here XYZ stands for a specific section name mentioned below, such as "Acknowledgements", "Dedications", "Endorsements", or "History".) To "Preserve the Title" of such a section when you modify the Document means that it remains a section "Entitled XYZ" according to this definition.

The Document may include Warranty Disclaimers next to the notice which states that this License applies to the Document. These Warranty Disclaimers are considered to be included by reference in this License, but only as regards disclaiming warranties: any other implication that these Warranty Disclaimers may have is void and has no effect on the meaning of this License.

2. VERBATIM COPYING

You may copy and distribute the Document in any medium, either commercially or noncommercially, provided that this License, the copyright notices, and the license notice saying this License applies to the Document are reproduced in all copies, and that you add no other conditions whatsoever to those of this License. You may not use technical measures to obstruct or control the reading or further copying of the copies you make or distribute. However, you may accept compensation in exchange for copies. If you distribute a large enough number of copies you must also follow the conditions in section 3.

You may also lend copies, under the same conditions stated above, and you may publicly display copies.

3. COPYING IN QUANTITY

If you publish printed copies (or copies in media that commonly have printed covers) of the Document, numbering more than 100, and the Document's license notice requires Cover Texts, you must enclose the copies in covers that carry, clearly and legibly, all these Cover Texts: Front-Cover Texts on the front cover, and Back-Cover Texts on the back cover. Both covers must also clearly and legibly identify you as the publisher of these copies. The front cover must present the full title with all words of the title equally prominent and visible. You may add other material on the covers in addition. Copying with changes limited to the covers, as long as they preserve the title of the Document and satisfy these conditions, can be treated as verbatim copying in other respects.

If the required texts for either cover are too voluminous to fit legibly, you should put the first ones listed (as many as fit reasonably) on the actual cover, and continue the rest onto adjacent pages.

If you publish or distribute Opaque copies of the Document numbering more than 100, you must either include a machine-readable Transparent copy along with each Opaque copy, or state in or with each Opaque copy a computer-network location from which the general network-using public has access to download using public-standard network protocols a complete Transparent copy of the Document, free of added material. If you use the latter option, you must take reasonably prudent steps, when you begin distribution of Opaque copies in quantity, to ensure that this Transparent copy will remain thus accessible at the stated location until at least one year after the last time you distribute an Opaque copy (directly or through your agents or retailers) of that edition to the public.

It is requested, but not required, that you contact the authors of the Document well before redistributing any large number of copies, to give them a chance to provide you with an updated version of the Document.

4. MODIFICATIONS

You may copy and distribute a Modified Version of the Document under the conditions of sections 2 and 3 above, provided that you release the Modified Version under precisely this License, with the Modified Version filling the role of the Document, thus licensing distribution and modification of the Modified Version to whoever possesses a copy of it. In addition, you must do these things in the Modified Version:

A. Use in the Title Page (and on the covers, if any) a title distinct from that of the Document, and from those of previous versions (which should, if there were any, be listed in the History section of the Document). You may use the same title as a previous version if the original publisher of that version gives permission.

B. List on the Title Page, as authors, one or more persons or entities responsible for authorship of the modifications in the Modified Version, together with at least five of the principal authors of the Document (all of its principal authors, if it has fewer than five), unless they release you from this requirement.

C. State on the Title page the name of the publisher of the Modified Version, as the publisher.

D. Preserve all the copyright notices of the Document.

E. Add an appropriate copyright notice for your modifications adjacent to the other copyright notices.

F. Include, immediately after the copyright notices, a license notice giving the public permission to use the Modified Version under the terms of this License, in the form shown in the Addendum below.

G. Preserve in that license notice the full lists of Invariant Sections and required Cover Texts given in the Document's license notice.

H. Include an unaltered copy of this License.

I. Preserve the section Entitled "History", Preserve its Title, and add to it an item stating at least the title, year, new authors, and publisher of the Modified Version as given on the Title Page. If there is no section Entitled "History" in the Document, create one stating the title, year, authors, and publisher of the Document as given on its Title Page, then add an item describing the Modified Version as stated in the previous sentence.

J. Preserve the network location, if any, given in the Document for public access to a Transparent copy of the Document, and likewise the network locations given in the Document for previous versions it was based on. These may be placed in the "History" section. You may omit a network location for a work that was published at least four years before the Document itself, or if the original publisher of the version it refers to gives permission.

K. For any section Entitled "Acknowledgements" or "Dedications", Preserve the Title of the section, and preserve in the section all the substance and tone of each of the contributor acknowledgements and/or dedications given therein.

L. Preserve all the Invariant Sections of the Document, unaltered in their text and in their titles. Section numbers or the equivalent are not considered part of the section titles.

M. Delete any section Entitled "Endorsements". Such a section may not be included in the Modified Version.

N. Do not retitle any existing section to be Entitled "Endorsements" or to conflict in title with any Invariant Section.

O. Preserve any Warranty Disclaimers.

If the Modified Version includes new front-matter sections or appendices that qualify as Secondary Sections and contain no material copied from the Document, you may at your option designate some or all of these sections as invariant. To do this, add their titles to the list of Invariant Sections in the Modified Version's license notice. These titles must be distinct from any other section titles.

You may add a section Entitled "Endorsements", provided it contains nothing but endorsements of your Modified Version by various parties—for example, statements of peer review or that the text has been approved by an organization as the authoritative definition of a standard.

You may add a passage of up to five words as a Front-Cover Text, and a passage of up to 25 words as a Back-Cover Text, to the end of the list of Cover Texts in the Modified Version. Only one passage of Front-Cover Text and one of Back-Cover Text may be added by (or through arrangements made by) any one entity. If the Document already includes a cover text for the same cover, previously added by you or by arrangement made by the same entity you are acting on behalf of, you may not add another; but you may replace the old one, on explicit permission from the previous publisher that added the old one.

The author(s) and publisher(s) of the Document do not by this License give permission to use their names for publicity for or to assert or imply endorsement of any Modified Version.

5. COMBINING DOCUMENTS

You may combine the Document with other documents released under this License, under the terms defined in section 4 above for modified versions, provided that you include in the combination all of the Invariant Sections of all of the original documents, unmodified, and list them all as Invariant Sections of your combined work in its license notice, and that you preserve all their Warranty Disclaimers.

The combined work need only contain one copy of this License, and multiple identical Invariant Sections may be replaced with a single copy. If there are multiple Invariant Sections with the same name but different contents, make the title of each such section unique by adding at the end of it, in parentheses, the name of the original author or publisher of that section if known, or else a unique number. Make the same adjustment to the section titles in the list of Invariant Sections in the license notice of the combined work.

In the combination, you must combine any sections Entitled "History" in the various original documents, forming one section Entitled "History"; likewise combine any sections Entitled "Acknowledgements", and any sections Entitled "Dedications". You must delete all sections Entitled "Endorsements."

6. COLLECTIONS OF DOCUMENTS

You may make a collection consisting of the Document and other documents released under this License, and replace the individual copies of this License in the various documents with a single copy that is included in the collection, provided that you follow the rules of this License for verbatim copying of each of the documents in all other respects.

You may extract a single document from such a collection, and distribute it individually under this License, provided you insert a copy of this License into the extracted document, and follow this License in all other respects regarding verbatim copying of that document.

7. AGGREGATION WITH INDEPENDENT WORKS

A compilation of the Document or its derivatives with other separate and independent documents or works, in or on a volume of a storage or distribution medium, is called an "aggregate" if the copyright resulting from the compilation is not used to limit the legal rights of the compilation's users beyond what the individual works permit. When the Document is included in an aggregate, this License does not apply to the other works in the aggregate which are not themselves derivative works of the Document.

If the Cover Text requirement of section 3 is applicable to these copies of the Document, then if the Document is less than one half of the entire aggregate, the Document's Cover Texts may be placed on covers that bracket the Document within the aggregate, or the electronic equivalent of covers if the Document is in electronic form. Otherwise they must appear on printed covers that bracket the whole aggregate.

8. TRANSLATION

Translation is considered a kind of modification, so you may distribute translations of the Document under the terms of section 4. Replacing Invariant Sections with translations requires special permission from their copyright holders, but you may include translations of some or all Invariant Sections in addition to the original versions of these Invariant Sections. You may include a translation of this License, and all the license notices in the Document, and any Warranty Disclaimers, provided that you also include the original English version of this License and the original versions of those notices and disclaimers. In case of a disagreement between the translation and the original version of this License or a notice or disclaimer, the original version will prevail.

If a section in the Document is Entitled "Acknowledgements", "Dedications", or "History", the requirement (section 4) to Preserve its Title (section 1) will typically require changing the actual title.

9. TERMINATION

You may not copy, modify, sublicense, or distribute the Document except as expressly provided under this License. Any attempt otherwise to copy, modify, sublicense, or distribute it is void, and will automatically terminate your rights under this License.

However, if you cease all violation of this License, then your license from a particular copyright holder is reinstated (a) provisionally, unless and until the copyright holder explicitly and finally terminates your license, and (b) permanently, if the copyright holder fails to notify you of the violation by some reasonable means prior to 60 days after the cessation.

Moreover, your license from a particular copyright holder is reinstated permanently if the copyright holder notifies you of the violation by some reasonable means, this is the first time you have received notice of violation of this License (for any work) from that copyright holder, and you cure the violation prior to 30 days after your receipt of the notice.

Termination of your rights under this section does not terminate the licenses of parties who have received copies or rights from you under this License. If your rights have been terminated and not permanently reinstated, receipt of a copy of some or all of the same material does not give you any rights to use it.

10. FUTURE REVISIONS OF THIS LICENSE

The Free Software Foundation may publish new, revised versions of the GNU Free Documentation License from time to time. Such new versions will be similar in spirit to the present version, but may differ in detail to address new problems or concerns. See http://www.gnu.org/copyleft/.

Each version of the License is given a distinguishing version number. If the Document specifies that a particular numbered version of this License "or any later version" applies to it, you have the option of following the terms and conditions either of that specified version or of any later version that has been published (not as a draft) by the Free Software Foundation. If the Document does not specify a version number of this License, you may choose any version ever published (not as a draft) by the Free Software Foundation. If the Document specifies that a proxy can decide which future versions of this License can be used, that proxy's public statement of acceptance of a version permanently authorizes you to choose that version for the Document.

11. RELICENSING

"Massive Multiauthor Collaboration Site" (or "MMC Site") means any World Wide Web server that publishes copyrightable works and also provides prominent facilities for anybody to edit those works. A public wiki that anybody can edit is an example of such a server. A "Massive Multiauthor Collaboration" (or "MMC") contained in the site means any set of copyrightable works thus published on the MMC site.

"CC-BY-SA" means the Creative Commons Attribution-Share Alike 3.0 license published by Creative Commons Corporation, a not-for-profit corporation with a principal place of business in San Francisco, California, as well as future copyleft versions of that license published by that same organization.

"Incorporate" means to publish or republish a Document, in whole or in part, as part of another Document.

An MMC is "eligible for relicensing" if it is licensed under this License, and if all works that were first published under this License somewhere other than this MMC, and subsequently incorporated in whole or in part into the MMC, (1) had no cover texts or invariant sections, and (2) were thus incorporated prior to November 1, 2008.

The operator of an MMC Site may republish an MMC contained in the site under CC-BY-SA on the same site at any time before August 1, 2009, provided the MMC is eligible for relicensing.

ADDENDUM: How to use this License for your documents

To use this License in a document you have written, include a copy of the License in the document and put the following copyright and license notices just after the title page:

```
Copyright (C)  year  your name.
Permission is granted to copy, distribute and/or modify this document
under the terms of the GNU Free Documentation License, Version 1.3
or any later version published by the Free Software Foundation;
with no Invariant Sections, no Front-Cover Texts, and no Back-Cover
Texts.  A copy of the license is included in the section entitled ``GNU
Free Documentation License''.
```

If you have Invariant Sections, Front-Cover Texts and Back-Cover Texts, replace the "with... Texts." line with this:

```
with the Invariant Sections being list their titles, with
the Front-Cover Texts being list, and with the Back-Cover Texts
being list.
```

If you have Invariant Sections without Cover Texts, or some other combination of the three, merge those two alternatives to suit the situation.

If your document contains nontrivial examples of program code, we recommend releasing these examples in parallel under your choice of free software license, such as the GNU General Public License, to permit their use in free software.

www.ingramcontent.com/pod-product-compliance
Lightning Source LLC
Chambersburg PA
CBHW062359220526
45472CB00008B/1866